g.

MINNEAPOLIS · ST. PAUL

A FUN-FILLED, FACT-PACKED TRAVEL & ACTIVITY BOOK

by Peg Helminski

D1556178

John Muir Publications

Santa Fe, New Mexico

Dedicated to my research assistant, Nate Helminski—
restaurant critic, tour taker, and play-structure tester.
He made this a fun book to write!   —P.H.

John Muir Publications,
P.O. Box 613, Santa Fe, New Mexico 87504

Printed in the United States of America.
First edition. First printing November 1996.

Library of Congress Cataloging-in-Publication Data
Kidding Around Minneapolis/St. Paul : a fun-packed, fact-filled,
travel & activity book / by Peg Helminski
    p.   cm.
    Includes indexes.
    Summary: Provides information on landmarks, museums,
parks, sports, activities, entertainment, restaurants, and more
things to see and do in Minneapolis and St. Paul.
    ISBN 1-56261-305-7 (pbk.)
    1. Minneapolis Region (Minn.)—Guidebooks—Juvenile lit-
erature. 2. Saint Paul Region (Minn.)—Guidebooks—Juvenile
literature. 3. Family recreation—Minnesota—Minneapolis
Region—Guidebooks—Juvenile literature. 4. Family recreation—Minnesota—Saint Paul Region—Guidebooks—Juvenile
literature [1. Minneapolis (Minn.)—Guides. 2. St. Paul
(Minn.)—Guides.] I. Title. II. Series.
F614.M6H45   1996
917.76'5790453—dc20   96-17041
                                      CIP
                                      AC

Editors Rob Crisell, Peggy Schaefer, Lizann Flatt
Production Nikki Rooker, Marie J.T. Vigil
Graphics Joanne Jakub
Typesetting Marie J.T. Vigil, Tamara Mallory
Activities Rob Crisell, Bobi Martin
Cover Design Caroline Van Remortel
Cover Photo Greater Minneapolis
Convention and Visitors Bureau
Back Cover Photo Greater Minneapolis
Convention and Visitors Bureau/
© Doug Beasley
Illustrations Stacy Venturi-Pickett
Maps Susan Harrison
Printer Burton & Mayer

Distributed to the book trade by
Publishers Group West
Emeryville, California

For photo credits, see page 139

C O N T E N T S

COLOR THE ROUTE
FROM YOUR HOMETOWN TO
MINNEAPOLIS OR ST. PAUL

If you're flying, color the states you'll fly over.
If you're driving, color the states you'll drive through.
If you live in Minnesota, color the states you have traveled to.

 WELCOME TO MINNEAPOLIS AND ST. PAUL!

YOU MIGHT THINK THAT MINNEAPOLIS and St. Paul are really one big city with one long name. Minneapolis and St. Paul—often called the Twin Cities, or "the Cities"—are actually two very different places. Both were shaped by what Native Americans called the Mississippi or the "Big River." The Mississippi doesn't separate Minneapolis from St. Paul, but instead winds through both cities. Directions here are given by the side of the Mississippi you're on. Even though it's in the southeast part of town, West St. Paul takes its name from its location on the west bank of the river. In this section you will discover other things besides the Mississippi that shaped these cities, such as their histories, industries, and famous citizens.

↑ St. Paul's skyline rises above the Mississippi River.

HOW TO USE THIS BOOK

Don't read this book straight through from cover to cover! Look through the Contents page for a chapter that interests you, or find a topic in the Index at the back. Skip around. Close your eyes, flip through a few pages, and point to a spot. Play a game. Check out the maps and make a list of all the cool stuff you want to see. Share interesting facts about Minneapolis and St. Paul with your family.

When you find something that interests you, flip to the Resource Guide toward the back of the book to find out where it is and when it's open. Then turn to the Geographic Index to find out what else you can see that's nearby. The Resource Guide also lists emergency information, extra sights that aren't described in this book, and places you can write to for maps and other information.

Minneapolis visitors admire the view from the Stone Arch Bridge. ↟

Though it's known as the Land of 10,000 Lakes, Minnesota actually has many more. At last count, the state had exactly 15,291 lakes.

ON THE GO!

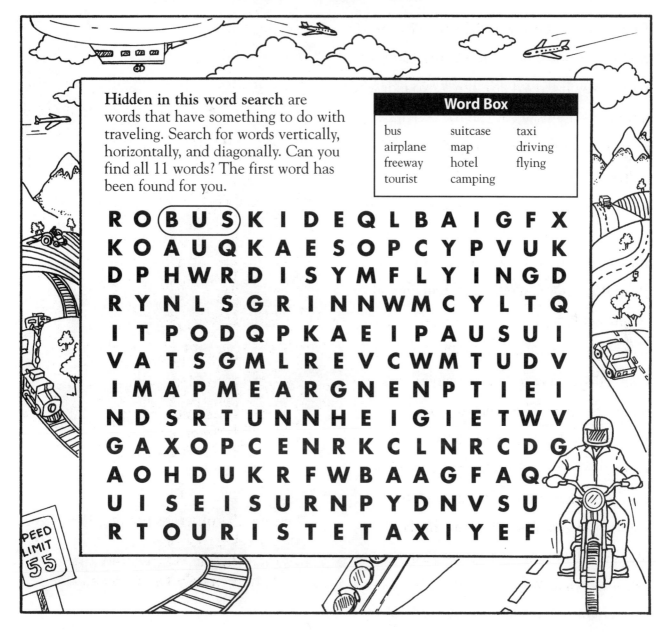

Hidden in this word search are words that have something to do with traveling. Search for words vertically, horizontally, and diagonally. Can you find all 11 words? The first word has been found for you.

Word Box

bus	suitcase	taxi
airplane	map	driving
freeway	hotel	flying
tourist	camping	

```
R O (B U S) K I D E Q L B A I G F X
K O A U Q K A E S O P C Y P V U K
D P H W R D I S Y M F L Y I N G D
R Y N L S G R I N N W M C Y L T Q
I T P O D Q P K A E I P A U S U I
V A T S G M L R E V C W M T U D V
I M A P M E A R G N E N P T I E I
N D S R T U N N H E I G I E T W V
G A X O P C E N R K C L N R C D G
A O H D U K R F W B A A G F A Q
U I S E I S U R N P Y D N V S U
R T O U R I S T E T A X I Y E F
```

A FRONTIER CITY

Minneapolis grew up around the Falls of St. Anthony, where the swift water powered sawmills and flour mills. The deeper water of the Mississippi River Gorge ended just above St. Paul. This was the last stop for steamboats from the south until 1850, when Governor Ramsey began to offer passage above the falls. Before the railroads arrived, steamboats delivered just about everything: food, clothing, the mail, and many immigrants.

The Cities are still growing rapidly. In 1990, the population of the capital city, St. Paul, was 272,000. Minneapolis, the state's largest city, was home to 368,000 residents. One reason for the growth might be that Minnesotans tend to live longer than people from other states in the U.S. The average life expectancy here is 76. Of all 50 states, only Hawaiians live longer. Today, the Cities are financial and manufacturing centers as well as cultural magnets for the whole state. Skyscrapers like the IDS Building and the World Trade Center tower over landmarks of the previous century like the Minneapolis City Hall clock tower.

It is considered good luck to rub the big toe (which is as big as an adult's whole hand) of the *Father of Waters* statue in the Minneapolis City Hall.

⬆ The Stone Arch Bridge leads into Minneapolis.

WEATHER WORRIES

If you want a variety of weather, Minnesota's got it! Winds on a typical January day can be cold enough to turn bare skin white with frostbite in just a few minutes. Still, Minnesotans enjoy their winters. Once the ice freezes to 12 inches thick, people drive their trucks onto the lakes, erect shelters, bore holes into the ice, and fish. Over the holes in the ice, people build "fish houses," which can be simple plastic tarps or small houses complete with stoves, bunk beds, carpeting, and TVs. For the less hearty, glass-enclosed passageways called skyways connect many downtown businesses with shopping areas and parking garages. Skyways cross the streets at the second- or third-floor building levels.

In springtime, parks, gardens, and prairies burst into flowers! Summers are usually pleasant, with temperatures in the

Winter in the Twin Cities can be long, cold, and snowy. ⚘

70s and 80s. However, 100-degree days, thunderstorms, tornadoes, and hailstorms are all possibilities. Autumn in the Twin Cities is a pleasure, with brisk, cool days and colorful leaves.

The Union Suit, a one-piece, full-body underwear, was invented in Minneapolis by George Munsing.

SEEING THE SIGHTS

There are many ways to enjoy the Cities. You can ride one of the trolleys or take a tour. On Saint Paul Gangster Tours, costumed guides offer inside information on the dark side of St. Paul's history. St. Paul offered mobsters like John Dillinger, Ma Barker, and Baby Face Nelson a special deal. The city agreed not to send criminals back to states where they were wanted by the police if they didn't commit crimes in Minnesota. See the sites of famous kidnappings, gunfights, and bank robberies. Another way to see the Cities is to take a riverboat ride. Stand on the deck behind the paddle wheel and feel it thump against the water as your face gets sprayed. Or, if you're going by foot with your family, walk to the mansions of St. Paul's Summit Avenue. The house of railroad baron **James J. Hill** is especially fun at Christmas. A holiday party at the Hill Mansion is reenacted by a cast of servants, and you become part of the story.

Master woodcarver Ian Kirchmeyer carved his likeness into a column in the James J. Hill Mansion. See how many times you can find his initials throughout the house.

← **The RiverCity trolley is a good way to see the Twin Cities.**

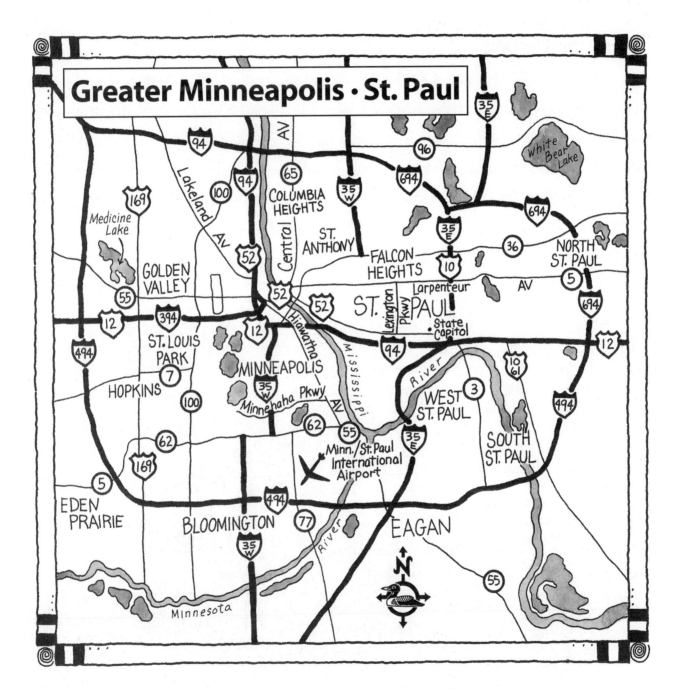

Greater Minneapolis · St. Paul

EARLY MINNESOTANS

Around 500 B.C., a people whom historians call Mound Builders settled here. Although hundreds of burial mounds have been destroyed over the years, several large mounds have been preserved at St. Paul's Indian Mounds Park. These people became the Dakota (which means "friend") and Ojibway. The Ojibway called themselves Anishinabe (ah-nee-shin-AH-bay), which means "the people." The Dakota village of Kaposia was on the site of present-day South St. Paul. Another village was at Lake Calhoun.

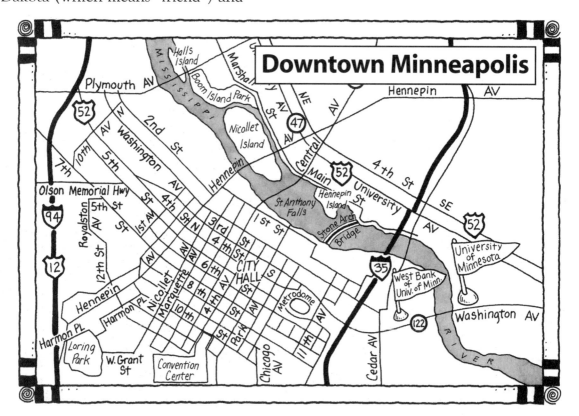

EUROPEANS ARRIVE

French fur trappers first came looking for beaver in the 1600s to make a type of hat that was popular at the time. In 1680, a French missionary named Father Louis Hennepin was adopted by a Dakota chief. He was the first white man to see the waterfalls the Ojibway called *Kakbikah*. Father Hennepin renamed them the Falls of St. Anthony. A second waterfall had been named *Minnehaha* ("curling waters") by the Dakota. We still use this name today.

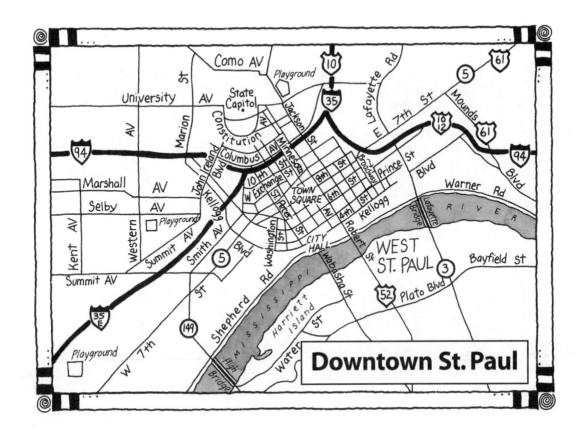

Downtown St. Paul

A Vacation in Pigseye?

Pierre Parrant opened a tavern on the banks of the Mississippi in 1838. Pierre was also known as "Pigseye," because a knife wound had left him with only one good eye. Pigseye was a criminal, and his tavern attracted other rough types. Mail even began to find its way to people staying at the tavern when addressed to "John Doe at Pigseye." Soon, everyone was calling the area near the tavern Pigseye.

Fortunately, Father Lucien Galtier built St. Paul's Church in 1841. People then began to call the area St. Paul's Landing, or St. Paul.

↑ Harriet Bishop was one of the first teachers in Minnesota.

The First Teacher

Imagine going to school in a chicken coop! That's what teacher Harriet Bishop's students did. Bishop moved from Vermont to an island in the Mississippi in 1847. Finding no other place to teach school, she turned a dark, log chicken coop and blacksmith shop into a one-room school house. Bishop's first challenge came when she discovered that her students spoke French and Dakota, while she spoke only English. Besides teaching, Bishop helped start St. Paul's first homeless shelter and worked for women's voting rights.

WHAT DOESN'T BELONG?

This is a scene that might have existed in St. Paul 150 years ago. Except here, you'll notice many things that didn't exist back then. When you find something that doesn't belong, circle it. Then color in the scene. Hint: There are at least 10 things that don't belong.

MINNEAPOLIS ON THE RISE

As the new capital grew, a treaty with the Indians opened the area around St. Anthony Falls for white settlement. Franklin Steele staked a claim and built a sawmill. He sold wood to the new settlers to build houses. People moved into the area so quickly that the wood didn't have time to dry properly after being cut. Sap often oozed from the walls of new houses! For a while, the city became known as Saint Anthony Falls. St. Anthony still exists as a neighborhood in Minneapolis.

Franklin Steele was responsible for St. Paul's early growth.

About 20 miles of caves and tunnels exist below St. Paul. Over many years, these tunnels have been used as homes, nightclubs, gangster hideouts, mushroom farms—they've even stored cheese!

INTERNATIONAL CITIES

Farmers from Sweden, Norway, and Denmark came to work the rich farmland west of the Mississippi. They called the area Minneapolis, meaning, "city of water." When lumber workers began to arrive from Maine, Minneapolis also became a booming lumber town. Sometimes the river was so jammed with logs that people could walk across the river by stepping from log to log.

WHAT'S THE DIFFERENCE?

These three photos of the *Pioneers* monument in downtown
St. Paul aren't exactly the same. Circle the photo that is different.

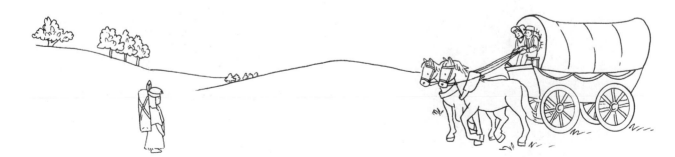

THE STONE ARCH BRIDGE

In 1879, a railroad bridge was proposed that would span the Mississippi River. Construction began in January 1882. In November 1883, railroad baron James J. Hill completed the only stone bridge to span the Mississippi. Those who thought the 2,100-foot-long bridge was impossible to build called it Jim Hill's Folly. But after it was finished, almost everyone called it an engineering marvel. Trains no longer cross this Minneapolis bridge, but you can walk or ride your bike across it to see St. Anthony Falls.

John Quincy Adams, named after our sixth U.S. president, was the editor of the Minneapolis-based newspaper *The Western Appeal*. Known as the national newspaper for African Americans, it helped the community become strong and organized.

NEIGHBORHOODS SHAPE CITIES

Bohemian Flats, Little Italy, Swede Hollow—these were the names of some of the Twin Cities' original neighborhoods on the flats. As you might have guessed, these neighborhoods were home to immigrants of different nationalities. Children once played in their narrow streets. Due to frequent flooding, however, none of these early neighborhoods exist today.

During the Vietnam War, Hmong (pronounced "mung") people from Laos performed dangerous missions for the U.S. Today, the Twin Cities host the largest urban settlement of Hmong in the nation.

DISASTERS STRIKE MINNEAPOLIS

Early settlers dug tunnels under St. Anthony Falls. This way, they could direct the water that powered the sawmills and flour mills. On October 5, 1869, people were awakened by the cry, "The falls are going out!" Water had eroded the soft limestone under the falls, and the tunnels were collapsing. The mills might have gone under, too, but people worked day and night to plug the holes. Finally, the government built a protective metal shield over the falls to support them. The mills were saved.

In 1878, the Washburn A Mill— "the finest flouring mill in the world"— exploded, killing 18 people and destroying five nearby mills.

⬆ **The Washburn Mill explosion**

Almost 25 years later, the C.A. Smith Sawmill caught fire. The fire spread through the East District of Minneapolis from 6th to 14th Streets and became a huge blazing pit. As one eyewitness reported, "The heat was so intense that the water from fire hoses turned to steam and went sailing skyward before it even reached the fire."

What the Twin Cities Mean to You

If you've ever used Scotch brand tape, a Post-it Note, or sandpaper, you've used an invention by a Minnesota's 3M Company. If you came by airplane to Minneapolis and St. Paul, perhaps you arrived on our own Northwest Airlines. Maybe the corn you ate last night for supper or the sunflowers you planted last summer came from seeds developed by research at Cargill. Your home heating

Created in Minnesota in 1921, Betty Crocker was never a real person. Nevertheless, for 24 years she had a show on the radio called *Cooking School of the Air*. She received 4,000 letters every day!

system may be controlled by a Honeywell thermostat. If you shop in a Target Store, Dayton's, or Hudson's, you are using a Minnesota business to meet your needs. And surely you must recognize two of our most famous "residents": Betty Crocker and the Pillsbury Doughboy.

⬆ **The Twin Cities are home to Northwest Airlines.**

⇡ Charles Schulz, a native of St. Paul, is famous for his *Peanuts* comic strip.

FAMOUS TWIN CITIES NATIVES

Little Crow watched as his people starved. The U.S. government had agreed to provide food, but it hadn't done anything. When he asked the settlers for food, they refused. Reluctantly, he led his people in the Dakota War of 1862. More than 55 settlers and soldiers died. After the fighting stopped, 38 Dakota men were hanged in Mankato, Minnesota, in the largest mass execution in American history.

Teacher and St. Paul resident Ann Bancroft reached the North Pole by dogsled in 1986. In 1993, she skied to the South Pole. More than 200,000 students followed her via computer linkup. Ann first learned about overcoming great obstacles in school, where she struggled with a learning disability called dyslexia.

Charles Schulz, the creator of Snoopy, Charlie Brown, and the *Peanuts* gang, was born in St. Paul. He learned how to draw cartoons from a correspondence course, where he received his worst grades for his drawings of children. Today, *Peanuts* appears in 2,000 newspapers all over the world.

Prince Rogers Nelson, the rock 'n' roll star formerly known as Prince, was born and still lives in Minneapolis.

PARKS AND THE GREAT OUTDOORS

THE TWIN CITIES' LAKES AREN'T JUST for looking at. In the early twentieth century, people decided that it was a good idea to preserve lands for public use as recreational areas and wildlife refuges. Minnesota, with its many lakes, was a leader in this movement. Public land was set aside so that wildlife could live undisturbed. Many parks were set up for both winter and summer use. Some of them now have swimming beaches, playgrounds, fishing piers, and boat rentals. Those who prefer a more relaxing vacation can take peaceful canoe rides around a few of the lakes. In winter, cross-country ski trails are everywhere. There are also a number of ice-skating rinks. Whatever the season, you can find what you want in Minneapolis and St. Paul.

⇑ Windsurfing on Lake Calhoun

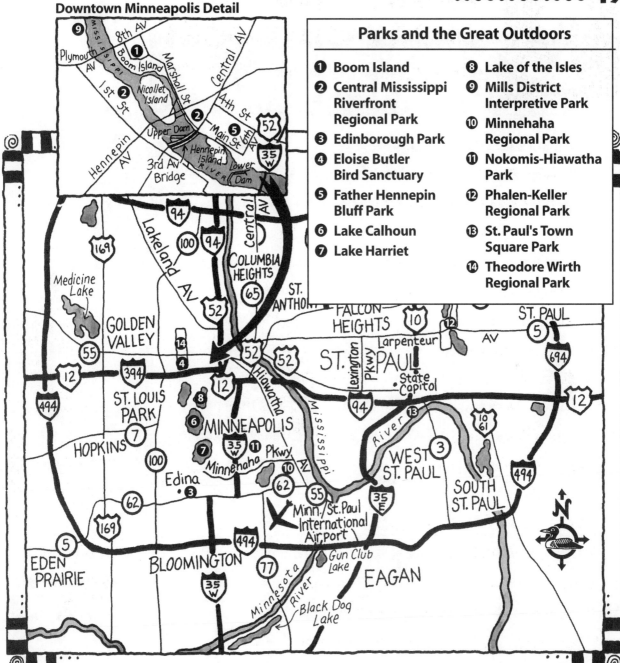

Downtown Minneapolis Detail

Parks and the Great Outdoors

❶ **Boom Island**

❷ **Central Mississippi Riverfront Regional Park**

❸ **Edinborough Park**

❹ **Eloise Butler Bird Sanctuary**

❺ **Father Hennepin Bluff Park**

❻ **Lake Calhoun**

❼ **Lake Harriet**

❽ **Lake of the Isles**

❾ **Mills District Interpretive Park**

❿ **Minnehaha Regional Park**

⓫ **Nokomis-Hiawatha Park**

⓬ **Phalen-Keller Regional Park**

⓭ **St. Paul's Town Square Park**

⓮ **Theodore Wirth Regional Park**

THEODORE WIRTH REGIONAL PARK

The largest of the Minneapolis regional parks, **Theodore Wirth Regional Park** includes the **Eloise Butler Bird Sanctuary,** the **J.D. Rivers 4-H Children's Garden,** a tamarack bog, the **Daylilly and Perennial Garden,** and a golf course. Some of the activities here are downhill and cross-country skiing, snow sledding, biking, skating, fishing, and swimming.

Established by Eloise Butler in 1907, the wildflower garden and bird sanctuary stretches over 14 acres. Hike the short nature trail and learn about four types of plant and animal habitats. Many songbirds and wading birds, such as the great blue heron and snowy egret, can be seen here. In early to mid-summer, the hills are covered with wildflowers. Butterflies are everywhere! Call ahead to find out when tours and nature programs will be offered.

⇞ **The tamarack bog at the Daylilly Perennial Garden**

⇞ **During the winter sledding is fun!**

A tamarack is a short-needled, North American tree grown for its beauty and for lumber.

HELP THE HIKERS!

start

Help the hikers find their way back to the picnic table.

CENTRAL MISSISSIPPI RIVERFRONT REGIONAL PARK

Boom Island was originally a holding place for logs until they were needed at the sawmill. When soil deposits built up, the island eventually turned into a peninsula.

On the west bank of the Mississippi, the Great River Road runs between Plymouth and Portland Avenues. Here you'll find walking and biking trails, the **Mills District Interpretive Park**, and the water-powered canal.

Boom Island, on the east bank between Eighth Avenue Northeast and Nicollet Island, is the largest riverfront park in Minneapolis. Picnic, walk along the river, or take a ride on the *Anson Northrup*. From Nicollet Island, you can get a good view of St. Anthony Falls and downtown Minneapolis. The amphitheater offers free concerts weekday evenings all summer.

Between Third Avenue Southeast and Hennepin Avenue is the town of St. Anthony's original **Main Street.** This area has been restored with cobblestones, brick walks, and old-style lighting. Nearby **Father Hennepin Bluff Park** offers excellent views of St. Anthony Falls, the downtown skyline, and more.

⬆
The sternwheeler *Anson Northrup* departs from Boom Island.

WHAT'S THE DIFFERENCE?

These two pictures of people on a river boat might look the same, but they're not. How many differences between the two scenes can you find?

MINNEAPOLIS CHAIN OF LAKES REGIONAL PARK

Three of the most popular Minneapolis parks are Lake Harriet, Lake Calhoun, and Lake of the Isles. **Lake of the Isles** is a wildlife refuge. Biking and hiking trails surround the water.

Lake Harriet is named for Harriet Leavenworth, wife of the first commander of Fort Snelling. Watch sailboat races in the afternoon and listen to a free concert on a summer evening at the **Lake Harriet Bandshell** (located on Lake Harriet and William Perry Parkway). Hop aboard the historic Lake Harriet streetcar for a scenic, two-mile ride to Lake Calhoun. This park also has a fishing dock, wild bird sanctuary, a rock garden, and a rose garden. During summer, concerts are held at the Lake Harriet Bandshell.

Lake Calhoun is a popular spot for fishing, skating, and boating. Before white settlers arrived, Native Americans lived at Lake Calhoun.

⬆ **Lake Harriet Bandshell sponsors concerts during the summer.**

On "Take a Kid Fishing Weekend," adults don't need a fishing license if they fish with someone who is 16 years old or younger.

⬆ **Northside Beach on Lake Calhoun is a popular place.**

PARK PUZZLE

Hidden in this word search are some things you might see or do at Minneapolis Chain of Lakes Regional Park. Search for words vertically, horizontally, and diagonally. Can you find all 11 words? The first word has been found for you.

Word Box		
hiking	garden	flowers
fish	concert	pond
birds	skating	bicycle
sailboat	park	

```
K O N A T K M E S O P M P A R K H
F P H F R D Q S Y M B E B A O N H
L Y N H A G A I N F I S H B L T F
O T P O I S S K A T R N G E L T D
W A T J G K N R D V D E L T R D G
E E U E M A I N G N S C G E Y E A
R D S R G T N N H U Y U C E B W R
S A N S P I I N G C C N M R A D D
P O N D U N R O I B O N T F L Q E
U I S E I G U B N C Y D N L L U N
R O T B L K I T E U L I M Y N F E
S A I L B O A T F R A P B X E Q R
```

NOKOMIS-HIAWATHA AND MINNEHAHA REGIONAL PARKS

This park surrounds Lake Hiawatha and Lake Nokomis. Water sports include sailboat racing, swimming, and fishing. You can also check out trails for biking, hiking, or roller skating. In winter, ice skating and cross-country skiing on lighted trails are popular.

Nearby is 142-acre **Minnehaha Regional Park**. The park's 53-foot **Minnehaha Falls** was the inspiration for Henry Wadsworth Longfellow's well-known poem "The Song of Hiawatha." Be sure to see the famous statue of Hiawatha and Minnehaha on the shores of the Minnehaha Creek. Also located here is the white farmhouse of John Stevens, the first settler in St. Anthony.

Bike, hike, or cross-country ski between various regional and city parks using the **Minnehaha Parkway**. This trail system connects Lake Harriet to Nokomis-Hiawatha Regional Park and Minnehaha Park.

⬆ *Hiawatha and Minnehaha* is the sculpture inspired by Henry Wadsworth Longfellow's famous poem.

⬅ **The Stevens House is in Minnehaha Regional Park.**

WRITE YOUR OWN POEM

Here are a few lines from Henry Wadsworth Longfellow's poem "The Song of Hiawatha." Write your own poem in the space provided.

Swift of foot was Hiawatha;
He could shoot an arrow from him,
And run forward with such fleetness,
That the arrow fell behind him!

_____

_____

_____

_____

_____

_____

PHALEN-KELLER REGIONAL PARK

⬆ **Having fun at Phalen-Keller Park's playground**

Ancient oak trees shade the paths where you can ride your bike, hike, or skate. In summer, play golf or spread out your towel on the white sands and take a swim at **Phalen Beach**. You and your family might want to rent a paddleboat or windsurfer. Or you might just want to play on the playground.

In winter, try your luck at Minnesota's coldest sport: ice fishing. Cross-country ski on four miles of groomed intermediate trails or skate on the ice rink. The trail system here connects to the **Keller Regional Park** and **Willard Munger State Trail**, which goes from St. Paul to Pine Point Park, about 18 miles away.

A chain of lakes, including Kohlman, Spoon, Gervais, Keller, Phalen, and Round, runs through the park.

In-line skates were invented in 1980 by Scott and Brennan Olson of Minneapolis.

⬆ **In-line skating by the lakes**

TRACE THE SKATERS

These kids skated out on the ice and left their boots behind. By tracing the tracks in the ice left by each skater, can you tell who each pair of boots belongs to?

INDOOR PARKS

⬆ **St. Paul's Town Square Park**

Cafesjian's Carousel was originally located at the state fair. Just when it was to be broken down and sold, St. Paul citizens banded together to save and restore it.

In a place with such long winters, there has to be somewhere to play when it's so cold that your breath forms icicles on your eyelashes! One of those places is **St. Paul's Town Square Park**. This multilevel park will make you think it's summer, even when it's not. Tropical plants and flowers are everywhere. Relax by an indoor waterfall or stop in at any of the nearby shops and restaurants. Of course, no visit here is complete without a ride on **Cafesjian's Carousel**. Colorful antique horses in high-spirited poses await your command.

If you have time, take a swim in the morning and ice skate in the afternoon at **Edinborough Park**, a fully enclosed one-acre park. Bring your lunch or buy one at the deli. Call ahead to find out what concerts or activities are scheduled.

Cafesjian's Carousel at St. Paul's Town Square Park ⬆

MY TRAVEL JOURNAL
—Parks and the Great Outdoors—

I had fun when I visited: _____

I learned about: _____

My favorite park was: _____

What I enjoyed doing the most was: _____

This is a picture of something I saw •••••

 ANIMALS AROUND THE TWIN CITIES

MINNESOTA IS HOME TO A STAGGERING NUMBER of wild animals. Flocks of Canada geese populate the Twin Cities' parks. Great blue herons and snowy egrets wade in ponds and streams. Bald eagles fish from chunks of ice that float down the Mississippi in early spring. Cottontail rabbits hop across lawns. Bats keep busy at night controlling the mosquitos, while white-tailed deer make dessert of rose gardens!

If you visit one of Minnesota's lakes, be on the lookout for muskrat, beaver, salamanders, frogs, turtles, and snakes. The walleye is the most popular game fish in Minnesota's lakes, but sunfish, crappies, brook and rainbow trout offer plenty of opportunities if you and your family enjoy fishing.

But if you don't feel like waiting for the animals to come to you, this section describes some places guaranteed to bring you to the animals.

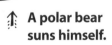

⇑ **A polar bear suns himself.**

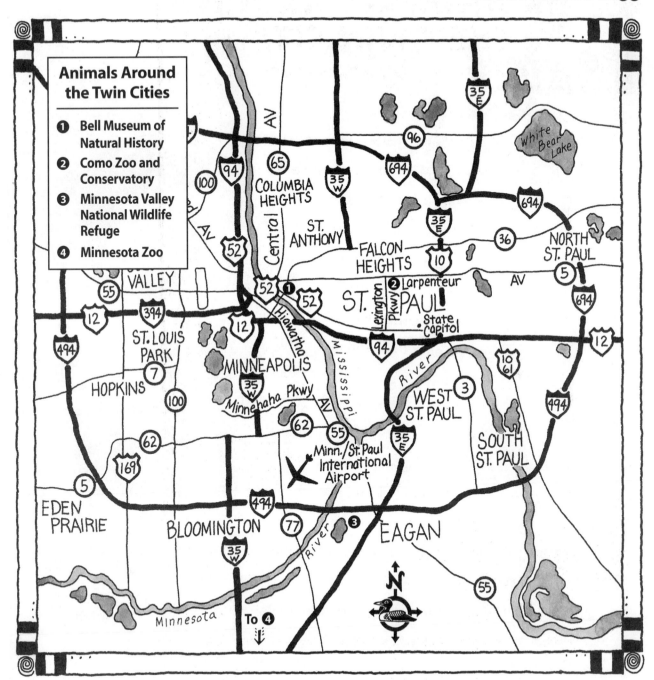

Animals Around the Twin Cities

❶ Bell Museum of Natural History
❷ Como Zoo and Conservatory
❸ Minnesota Valley National Wildlife Refuge
❹ Minnesota Zoo

COMO ZOO AND CONSERVATORY

Built in 1897, the Como Zoo is the least expensive place in the city to watch animals. You can see polar bears swim from the underwater viewing area or buy a cup of fish to feed the seals. During summer, be sure to get seats early for the **Sparky the Sea Lion Show.** You might want to play miniature golf, take a pony ride, or check out the amusement park. In the summer, be sure to take a dip in **Como Pool** and get "rained on" under the mushroom fountain in the splash pool.

At the conservatory, the tropical trees, plants, and seasonal flowers in the sunken garden room make you feel like it's summer, even on a cold winter day. If it is really winter, you might want to ski on a mile of lighted cross-country ski trails. New exhibits are scheduled to open soon.

⬆ Casey lives on Gorilla Island at the Como Zoo.

⬆ **Sparky performs for zoo visitors.**

On May 12, 1994, Casey, a 300-pound western lowland gorilla, jumped the moat around the Gorilla Island and took a tour of the zoo. Zookeepers soon built a higher wall.

CROSSWORD FUN

There is a lot to discover about the Como Zoo. Solve this crossword by figuring out the clues or completing the sentences. If you need help, use the clue box.

Across

2. You can get rained on under the mushroom _____ at the Como Zoo.
6. These cousins of the crocodile are coming to the Como Zoo soon.
7. This animal likes to bark and play with a ball. Its favorite snack is fish.
8. You like to look at the animals in the zoo, and they like to look at _____!

Down

1. You can ride these at the zoo. You might see them at a farm, too.
3. He's the star of Como Zoo's Sea Lion Show.
4. The king of the jungle.
5. These flying mammals hang out in caves all day.

MINNESOTA ZOO

More than 430 species of animals are exhibited within the zoo's 500 acres. Ride the monorail to see herds of buffalo grazing or tigers romping in the snow on a winter day. The giant coral reef at the end of the indoor **Tropics Trail** will leave you amazed—especially when zookeepers feed the sharks! In the **World of Birds** show, eagles swoop above your head, while a talking parrot keeps you laughing.

There are hands-on exhibits here, too. In the summer, you can feed the animals in the petting zoo. In the **Zoo Lab,** you're allowed to touch sea stars, chitons, snakes, chinchillas, and other animals.

In May 1997, the zoo will build a tide pool, a small shark and ray touch pool, a dolphin pool, and a large shark aquarium.

⇑ **Playful dolphins have found a home at the zoo.**

⇑ **There is a komodo dragon exhibit at the zoo.**

CONNECT THE DOTS

He can't breathe fire, but this dragon is a popular guest at the
Minnesota Zoo. Connect the dots, then color in the scene.

BELL MUSEUM OF NATURAL HISTORY

At the Bell Museum, you can discover what it feels like to touch a timber wolf or walk through a peat bog. You can get so close to these common—and rare—animals that you can even examine the color of their feathers and the shape of their feet. Preserved animals are displayed in dioramas showing their natural habitat. You can also visit the **Touch and See room** to feel different animal skins or peek through a microscope at some of the smallest wonders of our world. Here's the place to find out what you would look like if you had antlers! If you and your family are looking for a longer, more in-depth animal experience, try one of the week-long summer day camps or one-night overnights.

⇡ **What a giant bone!**

⇡ **Kids explore the Touch and See room.**

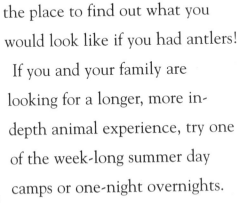

Once a bald eagle has caught its prey, it's nearly impossible for human hands to pry open its talons.

ord.” When all the blanks are filled in, read the story out loud. One of the blanks has been filled in for you.

Scott, _____, and I were leaving the Nature Center when we
         name

noticed some ___sticky___ tracks.
              describing word

"Do you think one of the animals got loose?" I asked.

"I hope it's not the _____," said Scott. "It's too
                     animal

_____!"
describing word

"I guess we'll never know unless we go _____," I said. So
                                        action word

we crept closer to the bushes until at last we noticed two eyes peering

out at us.

"_____!" I shouted. "It's just a _____."
   exclamation   thing

MINNESOTA VALLEY NATIONAL WILDLIFE REFUGE

This wildlife refuge is home (or at least a stopover) to 300 species of birds and animals. It's divided into three basic wildlife habitats: prairie, marshland, and hardwood. When you visit, plan to stop first at the visitors center. Watch the short slide program, "Minnesota Valley: A Place to Discover, A Place to Explore," and walk through the exhibits. Then put on your hiking shoes and go out to meet the native animals face-to-face. See if you can find a muskrat lodge. Look in the soft mud near the water's edge for animal tracks that you might recognize. If you don't want to miss anything, bring binoculars and a magnifying glass. Very few wildlife refuges like this one exist in U.S. cities.

Canadian geese and their young wander through the refuge.

Strange flowers like this one grow at the refuge.

If you see something slither past you in the city, relax! There are no poisonous snakes in the Twin Cities area.

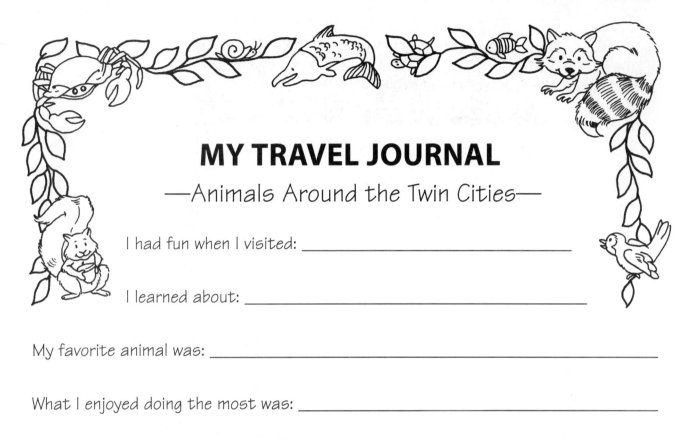

MY TRAVEL JOURNAL

—Animals Around the Twin Cities—

I had fun when I visited: _____

I learned about: _____

My favorite animal was: _____

What I enjoyed doing the most was: _____

This is a picture of an animal I saw

 LANDMARKS, SKYSCRAPERS, AND THE ARTS

IN EVERY CITY, THERE ARE CERTAIN buildings and statues that are so unique and well-loved that they can be called landmarks. Everyone knows these places. People give each other directions based on them: "Go three blocks south of the Capitol Building," or they might say, "Turn left after you pass the Foshay Tower."

Both Minneapolis and St. Paul have plenty of these interesting landmarks. In this section, you'll find out about some of the most famous ones.

⇑ **Modern skyscrapers tower over downtown Minneapolis.**

⇑
The Capitol Building in St. Paul

Downtown Minneapolis

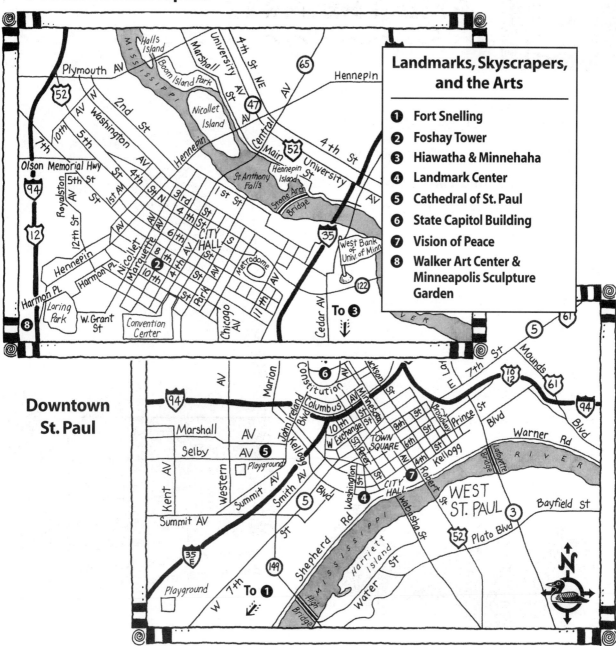

Landmarks, Skyscrapers, and the Arts

❶ **Fort Snelling**

❷ **Foshay Tower**

❸ **Hiawatha & Minnehaha**

❹ **Landmark Center**

❺ **Cathedral of St. Paul**

❻ **State Capitol Building**

❼ **Vision of Peace**

❽ **Walker Art Center & Minneapolis Sculpture Garden**

Downtown St. Paul

FOSHAY TOWER

The Foshay Tower is a 32-story, limestone-faced building built to resemble the Washington Monument. It was built in 1929 by millionaire Wilbur B. Foshay, who came to Minneapolis in 1915 and made a fortune in utilities. The interior featured Italian marble walls, delicate chandeliers, and a gold- and silver-plated ceiling. John Philip Sousa and his 75-piece band played at the building's opening, which included a show of fineworks and meals for 25,000 leaders, celebrities, and investors, and fireworks. Two months after his building was completed, Foshay lost everything in the stock-market crash. Later, he was found guilty of mail fraud and spent three years in prison.

⇑ **During its time, the Foshay Tower was one of the most amazing skyscrapers in the U.S.**

The Foshay Tower was the tallest building in Minneapolis until the IDS Building was built in 1972. You can still enjoy a spectacular view of Minneapolis from Foshay's observation deck.

⇑ **John Philip Sousa performed at the opening of the Foshay Tower.**

COLOR THE SCENE

Foshay Tower (with the spire on top of its pyramid roof) was the tallest building in Minneapolis until 1972.

HISTORIC FORT SNELLING

Historic Fort Snelling became a center for culture, supplies, and information for early travelers. Once known as Fort St. Anthony, Fort Snelling received its new name in 1925, from its first commander, Colonel Josiah Snelling. The hexagonal tower inside the fort is one of the oldest buildings in the state.

Life here was far from luxurious. Fort Snelling was the last outpost to the unexplored frontier. Soldiers slept two to a bunk, head to toe. The laundress washed their white uniforms in a kettle of boiling water. Often, Indians camped outside the walls and traded furs to settlers. Today, costumed guides reenact these roles. On Children's Day, take part in the wooden musket drill or help ready the cannon for firing.

↑ **Colonel Josiah Snelling**

To get through a typical winter, Fort Snelling required a stack of fire wood four feet high, four feet wide, and two miles long!

⇐
A cannon booms at Fort Snelling.

WHAT'S WRONG HERE?

Strange things are happening at Fort Snelling today.
Circle at least 15 things you think are wrong with this picture.
When you're done, color the scene.

MINNESOTA STATE CAPITOL BUILDING

↓ **The dome of the Capitol Building**

Modeled after the nation's Capitol in Washington, D.C., Minnesota's Capitol Building has the largest unsupported marble dome in the world. Building materials include marble, Minnesota granite, sandstone, and red pipestone.

The sculpture of four horses pulling a chariot is called *Quadriga*. The two women leading the horses are named "Agriculture" and "Industry." The four horses represent the forces of nature: earth, wind, fire, and water. Completely covered in gold, the sculpture symbolizes progress and prosperity in Minnesota.

If you stop at the visitor information desk, you can pick up a copy of the brochure "Art Treasures in the Capitol" for $1. Try to complete the treasure-hunt guide and become a certified junior art historian. The tour itself is free. The guides will tell you about the building's artworks, plus the history of Minnesota.

↑ **In 1979, Minnesotan Rosalie Wahl became the first female state supreme court justice.**

WHAT'S IN COMMON?

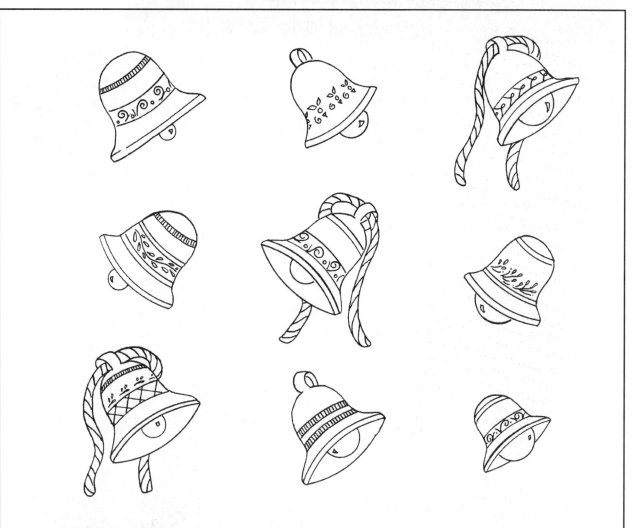

**Each of these bells has something in common with the other two in the same row.
For example, the three bells in the top row are all moving in the same direction. Draw
a line through each row and describe what the bells in that row have in common.
Don't forget to include diagonals!**

CATHEDRAL OF ST. PAUL

With seating for 3,000 people, the 306-foot-tall Cathedral of St. Paul is one of the largest church buildings in North America. From the outside, the granite church resembles St. Peter's Cathedral in Rome. Inside and behind the main altar is a semicircle of smaller altars called the **Shrines of the Nations.** Each is dedicated to a national patron saint of the different people who settled the city of St. Paul.

The copper-domed cathedral is actually the fourth church in the city named for St. Paul. In 1841, Father Lucien Galtier built a chapel of wood overlooking the Mississippi River. In 1851, a brick structure took its place. Seven years later, the Catholic community in the area had grown so rapidly that a larger church was needed. A stone church replaced the brick one. In 1904, Archbishop John Ireland began building the present cathedral. Archbishop Ireland actively encouraged Catholics to settle in Minnesota. To this day, Minnesota is still mostly Catholic.

Together, the bells in the cathedral's tower weigh 17,515 pounds— about as much as 4½ minivans!

The Cathedral of St. Paul from the air

CONNECT THE DOTS

Ice carving is a favorite pastime of people from Minneapolis and St. Paul. Connect the dots to see what ice sculpture is pictured here, then color in the scene.

LANDMARK CENTER

The five-story, granite Landmark Center is the closest thing to a castle in St. Paul. The building was built as a federal court house, post office, and customs clearinghouse. It was the site of famous gangster trials were held there in the 1920s and 1930s. The head of the FBI, J. Edgar Hoover, escorted notorious villain Alvin "Kreepy" Karpis there for his trial.

When the federal staff outgrew the building in 1967 and moved its offices to a new location, the Landmark Center was scheduled for demolition. Because of its unique architecture and historic importance, citizens banded together to save and restore it. Today, it houses cultural centers such as the **Museum of American Art** and the **Schubert Club Museum of Musical Instruments.**

⇑ **Known for its graceful towers, the Landmark Center once was a federal courthouse.**

⇐ **Kids at the St. Paul Winter Carnival, held near the Landmark Center**

During the Winter Carnival, Rice Park is the site of the ice sculpture competition. Whole scenes are sculpted in giant blocks of ice.

LOST IN THE SCULPTURE GARDEN

Start

EXIT →

Can you help the two kids find their way out of the sculpture garden?
When you're done with the maze, color in the scene.

WALKER ART CENTER & MINNEAPOLIS SCULPTURE GARDEN

The sculpture *Hare on Bell on Portland Stone Piers*

The Walker is named after Thomas Barlow Walker, a lumber baron who established the first art gallery in the area in 1879. The current building was opened in 1971 and expanded in 1984. In some rooms you can put on headphones and listen to music that was popular when some of the paintings you're looking at were created. Throughout the Walker, you can slip into mini-theaters or computer booths to learn more about the artists or art period displayed nearby. Don't forget to visit the sculpture garden while you're at the museum. You can wander outdoors, and around every turn in the hedge, another artistic surprise awaits. The sculpture garden is open year-round, though snow boots are essential equipment during winter.

Spoon Bridge and Cherry, the fountain sculpture in the Walker's garden, is often used as a symbol for Minneapolis.

HIDE AND SEEK!

Draw circles around all 16 hidden objects in this drawing. When you're done, color in the scene. Look for a face, wrench, cup, plunger, pencil, skateboard, bell, truck, book, bat, ruler, iron, apple, four-leaf clover, hamburger, and hot dog.

A sculpture of an eagle watches over St. Paul.

Hiawatha and Minnehaha **was partially funded by children who donated $1,000 in pennies.**

ART ON THE LOOSE

In Minneapolis at Fifth Avenue Northwest and Marshall Street stands John K. Daniels' statue showing three generations of a pioneer family. In Loring Park, Jacob Fjelde's statue of Norwegian violinist Ole Bull impresses visitors with its strength and beauty.

St. Paul has its own share of interesting monuments. At Fourth and Jackson Streets, the eagle statue that originally stood in front of the New York Life Insurance Building on Minnesota Street in St. Paul was eventually sold to the city.

The Vision of Peace in city hall is the largest carved black onyx figure in the world. Designed by Swedish sculptor Carl Milles, it depicts Native Americans smoking peace pipes. The 60-ton, 36-foot-high statue slowly rotates on a turntable.

Another statue of Jacob Fjelde's rests just above Minnehaha Falls. It is a statue called *Hiawatha and Minnehaha*, two Native American sweethearts.

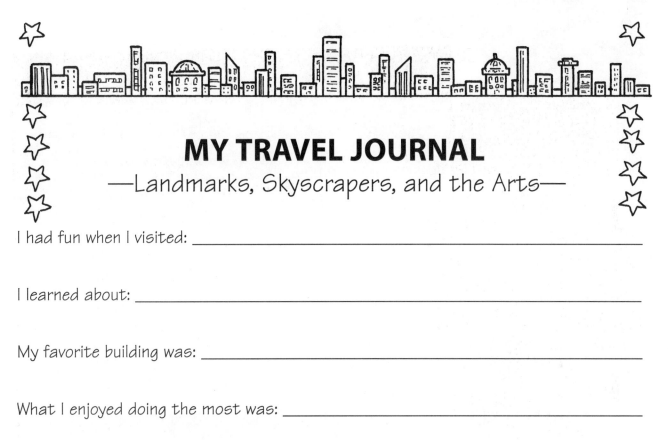

MY TRAVEL JOURNAL
—Landmarks, Skyscrapers, and the Arts—

I had fun when I visited: _____

I learned about: _____

My favorite building was: _____

What I enjoyed doing the most was: _____

This is a picture of a landmark or building I saw

GOOD SPORTS

WHETHER IT'S BASEBALL, FOOTBALL, basketball—or even roller hockey—you can find it in the Twin Cities. Professional teams include the Minnesota Twins, the Vikings, the Timberwolves, the Thunder (soccer), and the Arctic Blast (roller hockey).

⇡ **The Twins play baseball inside the Minneapolis Metrodome.**

If you would rather play sports than watch them, there are plenty of opportunities for that, too. Festivals like the summer Aquatennial in Minneapolis and the Winter Carnival in St. Paul have some exciting competitions: speed skating, softball on the surface of a frozen lake, running, or rowing across a lake in a boat made of milk cartons!

You can also try out one of the many skating rinks, indoor sports centers, or mini-golf courses. For more information, check the Resource Guide.

⇡ **Rowers at the Milk Carton Boat Race in Minneapolis**

Good Sports

1. All Seasons Golf Dome
2. Bloomington Ice Garden
3. Golf Mountain
4. Grand Slam Sports
5. Hubert H. Humphrey Metrodome
6. Inside Sports
7. Lava Links
8. P.J. Asch Outfitters

HUBERT H. HUMPHREY METRODOME

The Metrodome is home to the Minnesota Twins, the Vikings, and the University of Minnesota Golden Gophers football team. Named after one of Minnesota's most famous politicians, it was completed in 1981, cost $62 million, and seats 63,000. The Teflon-coated dome is two layers of fiberglass fabric (weighing one pound per square inch) separated by a pocket of air. The dome was first inflated on October 2, 1981. But what goes up does not always stay up! The dome has collapsed several times due to heavy snow or high winds.

Games are won and lost because of balls caught in light fixtures and heating ducts. In 1984, Dave Kingman of the Oakland A's hit a high pop fly. The ball disappeared through the seven-inch hole in the center of the dome. Kingman was awarded a "roof-rule" double.

Warren Moon drops back for a pass for the Minnesota Vikings.

⇐ You can see the Minneapolis skyline behind the Metrodome.

Between sporting events, the Metrodome becomes the Rollerdome, the world's largest skating facility.

MIXED-UP PICTURE STORY

It's going, going, gone! Put the scene in the correct order by filling in the number box in the bottom right-hand corner of each picture.

SPORTS CENTERS

If you're tired of warming the bench, here are some places you can go to get active!

At **Grand Slam Sports**, play mini-golf, perfect your batting swing, run off steam in the play zone, or team up for a round of laser tag. Love baseball? Check out **Inside Sports**. You can work on your hitting and fielding skills or take part in a baseball or softball clinic. If you like to ice skate, sharpen your blades and head for the **Bloomington Ice Garden**. This facility has three ice rinks.

Want to try something different? Improve your concentration and think your way higher than ever before. **P.J. Asch Outfitters**, in Stillwater, used to be a grain elevator, but now it's an indoor climbing wall. You can also rent whatever equipment you need for outdoor adventures here, too.

The climbing wall at P.J. Asch Outfitters

Ice skating is very popular in Minneapolis. ⇛

CROSSWORD FUN

Solve this sports crossword by figuring out the clues or completing the sentences. If you need help, use the clue box.

Clue Box		
safe	indoors	laser
golf	bat	ball
events	ice skates	good sport

Across

2. When it's cold or raining outside you must play _____.
5. You can play tag in the dark with this beam of light.
6. If you're hitting a small ball around an obstacle course, you're probably playing miniature _____.
7. You can get one of these made of plastic, wood, or metal.
8. In sports, games are also called sporting _____.

Down

1. Whether you win or lose you should be a _____ (two words).
2. At the Bloomington Ice Garden there are three places to use these (two words).
3. If you make it to first base before the ball gets there, you're _____.
4. You need one of these to play baseball, football, or soccer.

St. Paul native Patty Berg won 55 tournaments. ⇓

GOLFING THROUGH THE TWIN CITIES

Many golfers start out by playing miniature golf. When you think of mini-golf, you probably imagine warm summer evenings, right? Well, in Minneapolis and St. Paul, you can play golf year-round. **Lava Links** is an indoor 18-hole course in Minneapolis. It has real sand traps, a scary-looking volcano, waterfalls, and lava pits. Arcade games and laser tag are also available. Located on the opposite side of the Cities, **Golf Mountain** is the largest 18-hole miniature golf course in the United States. This multilevel course begins on the third floor of the Mall of America.

In Minnesota, there are more golf courses per person than in any other state. Many parks have public courses for those who own clubs. If you and your parents are serious about learning the game, you can buy a bucket of balls and rent some kid-size clubs at **All Seasons Golf Dome**.

⇐ **Going for a hole in one at Gold Mountain**

WHICH IS THE SAME?

This miniature golf course has nine holes, but only two of them are exactly alike. When you've circled the holes that are the same, color in the scene.

Speed skater Bonnie Blair is all smiles after winning her fifth Olympic gold medal.

The Twins' Kirby Puckett retired in 1996.

SOME FAMOUS ATHLETES

Fran Tarkenton was the first Viking player to make the Pro Football Hall of Fame. He completed 3,686 passes for 47,003 yards and 342 touchdowns. He is one of the greatest quarterbacks of all time.

Speed skater **Bonnie Blair** has been competing nationally since she was 16, skating her first race at age four. In 1994, she won two Olympic gold medals at the Lillehammer games in Norway, bringing her career total to five Olympic gold medals, more than any other American woman athlete has ever claimed.

In 1996, an eye disease called glaucoma forced **Kirby Puckett,** Minnesota's favorite baseball player, into retirement. Puckett is admired for both his offensive and defensive skills. In 1989, he led the American League with a batting average of .339. He won six Golden Glove awards for his fielding skills and played in two World Series.

MY TRAVEL JOURNAL
—Good Sports—

I had fun when I visited:

_____

I learned about: _____

My favorite sport is: _____

I like it because: _____

What I enjoyed doing the most was: _____

This is a picture of something I saw

6 MUSEUMS AND MORE

ARE YOU INTERESTED IN AFRICAN ART? Weird medical devices from long ago? Outer space and stars? You're in luck! The Twin Cities boast museums for each one of these interests. Several museums have things you can try out for yourself, like the ones in the "Touch and See" room at Gibbs Farm and in many of the experiments at the Science Museum. You can even have your scalp bumps interpreted at the Museum of Questionable Medical Devices.

Museum guides are eager to answer questions and share interesting facts about the exhibits. Some of the best places for kids are described in this section. A few more are listed in the Resource Guide in the back.

⬆ The American Swedish Institute looks like a castle.

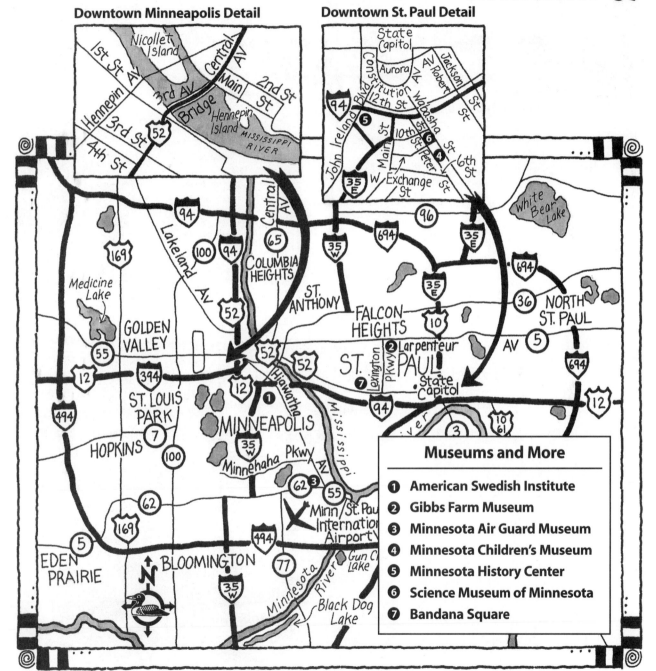

Downtown Minneapolis Detail

Downtown St. Paul Detail

Museums and More

1. American Swedish Institute
2. Gibbs Farm Museum
3. Minnesota Air Guard Museum
4. Minnesota Children's Museum
5. Minnesota History Center
6. Science Museum of Minnesota
7. Bandana Square

MINNESOTA AIR GUARD MUSEUM

↓ **The F-4** *Phantom*

The airfield at the Minnesota Air Guard Museum began as a racetrack. In the early part of this century, few airports existed. So, daring pilots—called barnstormers—landed wherever they found smooth ground. They flew from one rural area to another, thrilling audiences with aerial tricks like barrel rolls and wing walking. This white, oval racetrack was an easily recognizable landmark from 50 miles away. The grassy infield was the perfect place to land a plane.

On that same airfield today, you can see historic airplanes. Some early airplanes look like motorcycles sandwiched between two wings. Imagine how you would have felt trying to push those flying machines off the ground! Or picture yourself cruising high over enemy territory at the controls of the stealth spy plane, the A-12 *Blackbird*.

The CIA's A-12 *Blackbird* **holds the world's speed record. In 1990, this spy plane reached Mach 3.45— almost four times faster than a passenger plane.**

↓ **The F-101** *Voodoo*

DANGEROUS DAN

Without telling anyone what you're doing, ask for a word to fill in each blank. For example, "Give me an action word." When the blanks have been filled in, read the story out loud. One blank has been done for you.

Jacob loved to _____ with Dangerous Dan the Daredevil
                  action word

Flyer. Over _____ and around _____ they flew. Dan flew
              things   things

the loop-the-loop and the barrel _____ . Sometimes, people
                                   action word

came out of their _____ to watch. Jacob thought they looked
                    things

like _____ ants _____ing around on the ground.
      describing word   action word

    Once, Dan flew past a flock of **elephants** . Jacob pretended
                                        animals

he was one of them. At the end of the ride, Dangerous Dan let

Jacob back the _____ plane into the _____. Jacob
                color   thing

can't wait until he is old enough to be a pilot like Dangerous Dan!

AMERICAN SWEDISH INSTITUTE

In 1850, only four people from Sweden were living in Minnesota. By 1900, there were over 100,000. In fact, by the end of the nineteenth century, about 1,250,000 Swedes—one quarter of the total population of Sweden—had emigrated to America.

A sod house on the prairie in America gave Swedes a chance to own land—something most of them couldn't do in Europe.

Some immigrant Swedes did become rich. One was millionaire newspaper publisher named Swan Turnblad. His home (which looks like a castle) is now the American Swedish Institute. On a self-guided tour of the institute, you can see the kinds of books, musical instruments, toys, and tools immigrant families brought from Sweden a century ago. If you're hungry, sample Swedish pastries in the museum's coffee shop. There's a variety of activities throughout the year. Who knows? You might be asked to help other kids perform Swedish folk dances.

Swedish immigrant Swan Turnblad (shown here with his family) became a Twin Cities millionaire.

Immigrant families from Sweden packed everything they owned into an "America trunk." Children were permitted to bring only one or two small toys.

MIXED-UP PICTURE STORY

Many Swedes came to America during the nineteenth century. Put the scene in the correct order by filling in the number box in the bottom right-hand corner of each picture.

GIBBS FARM MUSEUM

At Gibbs Farm Museum, you can step back in time and find out for yourself what farm life was like in the 1800s. Learn how to make soap, churn butter, and crank an ice-cream freezer. In the farmhouse, everything is just as Heman and Jane Gibbs left it. Costumed guides answer your questions and demonstrate how kids did certain chores. You can try out a variety of old tools for yourself and figure out what they were used for in the **Touch and See room**. Learn about different kinds of farm animals in the white barn. (While you're there, don't forget to feed the chickens!) You can also join in on plenty of live demonstrations and activities. They vary with the day and season—just as farm life does.

A girl pets a horse at Gibbs Farm.

In the 1800s, naughty students had to press their noses against a chalk circle on the blackboard. If the circle smudged, the teacher knew they had moved.

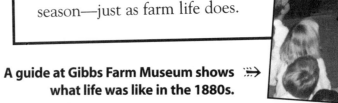

A guide at Gibbs Farm Museum shows ⇛ what life was like in the 1880s.

DOWN ON THE FARM

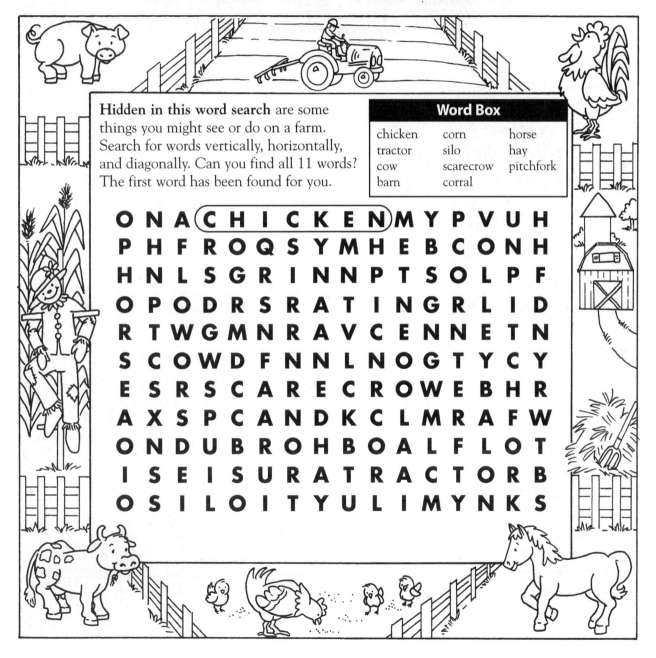

Hidden in this word search are some things you might see or do on a farm. Search for words vertically, horizontally, and diagonally. Can you find all 11 words? The first word has been found for you.

Word Box

chicken	corn	horse
tractor	silo	hay
cow	scarecrow	pitchfork
barn	corral	

```
O  N  A  C  H  I  C  K  E  N  M  Y  P  V  U  H
P  H  F  R  O  Q  S  Y  M  H  E  B  C  O  N  H
H  N  L  S  G  R  I  N  N  P  T  S  O  L  P  F
O  P  O  D  R  S  R  A  T  I  N  G  R  L  I  D
R  T  W  G  M  N  R  A  V  C  E  N  N  E  T  N
S  C  O  W  D  F  N  N  L  N  O  G  T  Y  C  Y
E  S  R  S  C  A  R  E  C  R  O  W  E  B  H  R
A  X  S  P  C  A  N  D  K  C  L  M  R  A  F  W
O  N  D  U  B  R  O  H  B  O  A  L  F  L  O  T
I  S  E  I  S  U  R  A  T  R  A  C  T  O  R  B
O  S  I  L  O  I  T  Y  U  L  I  M  Y  N  K  S
```

MINNESOTA CHILDREN'S MUSEUM

Trying out the wall of pins at the museum

Almost everything at this new museum is designed to be touched, climbed on, or moved around. The Minnesota's Children's Museum is really a three-story play space, where you learn while you play. Most exhibits are set up so that kids of different ages can experience them, but each learns something unique. Climb through a giant maze of tunnels and chambers to see what life is like for ants. Operate a crane. Float boats down a waterfall. Bounce a laser beam off mirrors. You can even see who can make the coolest face in a giant wall of pins! Some of the activities need more than one person to make them work. The huge air-powered band, for instance, requires at least one person to pedal fast enough to produce air for the instruments while another person presses buttons to make them play.

Experimenting with one of the museum's hands-on science activities ⇨

HIDE AND SEEK!

Draw circles around all 17 hidden objects in this drawing. When you're done, color in the scene. Look for a fish, paintbrush, apple, cup, iron, flower, fox's head, pencil, camera, mushroom, bell, duck's head, ruler, book, wool cap, screwdriver, rabbit's head.

MINNESOTA HISTORY CENTER

Have you ever seen a grain elevator and wondered how it worked? The Minnesota History Center lets you climb inside of one and walk through a maze. It's just one of the ways you can see what it was like to be a farmer in Minnesota. Relive the famous meat packing house strike of 1948. Use a Photo Find Ring from the **Gallery Games Kiosk** to take a treasure hunt. Some guides demonstrate how to paddle a fur trapper's canoe or gather wild rice like the Ojibway Indians did. Be sure to save time for the dramatic multimedia show *Home Place Minnesota*. It's full of trapdoors and surprises.

The museum holds special activities throughout the year. You can listen to African American folk tales or Native Americans singing a drum song. There is so much to do here that you won't want to leave.

↑ **Storytelling at the History Center**

↑ **The Minnesota History Center building is very modern looking.**

COLOR TO FIND THE ANSWER

Many early explorers used this type of boat to navigate rivers and creeks. Color the shapes with numbers brown. Color the shapes with letters blue. If a shape doesn't have a letter or number, use any color you want.

SCIENCE MUSEUM OF MINNESOTA

Visitors at the Science Museum learn how a ⇓ tornado forms.

Where can you play music just by walking up and down the stairs, or watch molten lava form into rock before your eyes? You can do this and more at the Science Museum of Minnesota. If you had time, you could spend days playing with the experiments, looking at exhibits, or watching scientists clean dinosaur bones in the fossil room. You and your family are encouraged to try things out.

Be sure to check out the **Omnitheater** show. Surrounded by a giant screen and stereo sound, you'll actually have the feeling of being part of the action. You might run with a herd of wildebeest across the Serengeti, or fly through space with an American astronaut.

Meet Iggy, the 40-foot-long iguana, at the entrance to the Science Museum. Iggy was sculpted out of 12,500 railroad spikes by teenager Nick Swearer.

Playing with a science exhibit at the museum

CONNECT THE DOTS

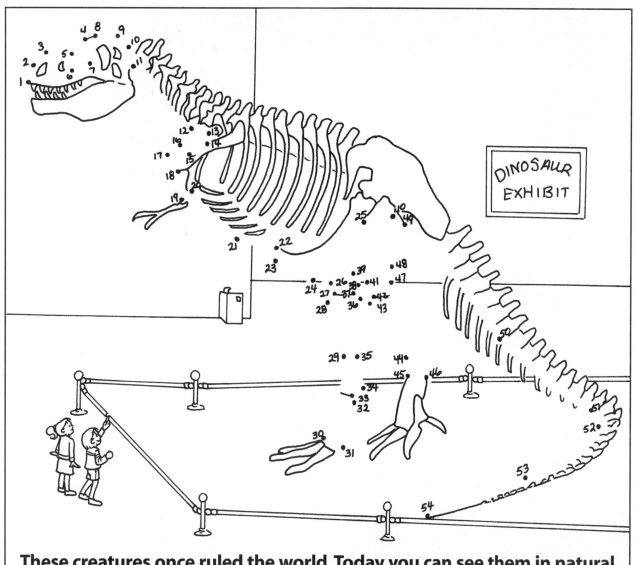

These creatures once ruled the world. Today you can see them in natural history museums. Connect the dots, then color in the scene.

TRAINS AT BANDANA SQUARE

If you love model trains—and even if you think you don't—you need to see the trains on the second floor of Bandana Square shopping mall. The model train set in the mall is twice as big as the average American home. Run by the Twin City Model Railroad Club, it includes scale models of the Stone Arch Bridge and many other landmarks throughout Minneapolis and St. Paul. Trains and trolleys of all different colors, ages, and sizes motor through miniature scenes of life in the old days. Look for the miniature junk in the junkyard! Watch the trains circle around the track. On special days, train operators dim the overhead lights, making the whole model glow with the lights of the trains and miniature buildings.

Bandana Square was once called the Como Shops. It was a place where trains were repaired. You can still see many old train engines and railroad cars on display outside.

Kids at Bandana Square watch as model trains speed by.

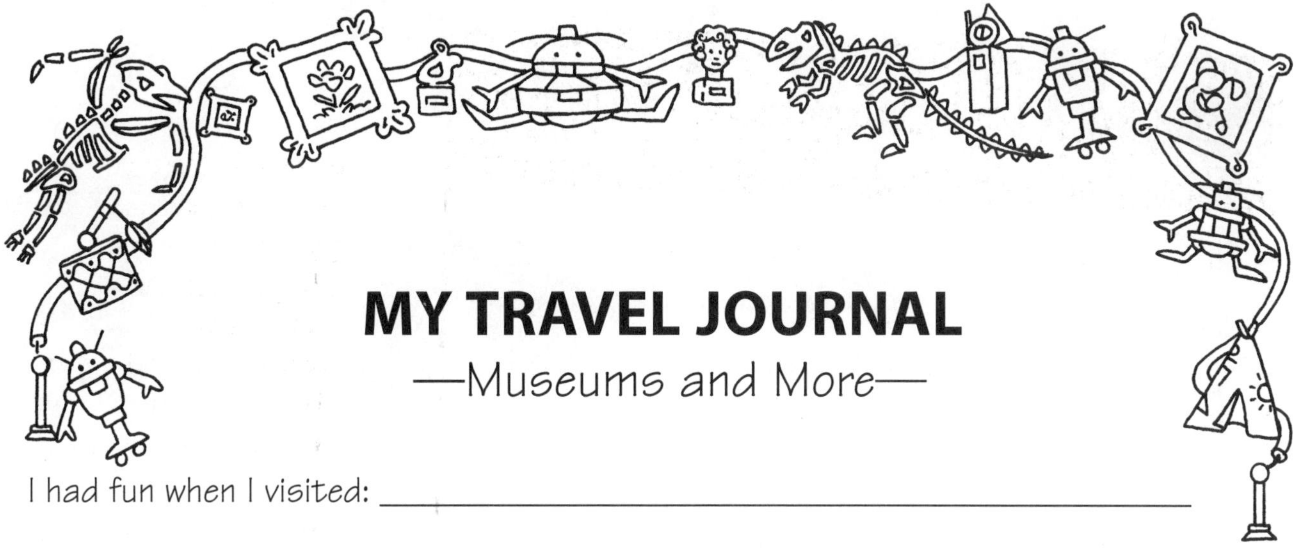

MY TRAVEL JOURNAL
—Museums and More—

I had fun when I visited: _____

My favorite museum was: _____

What I enjoyed doing there the most was: _____

I learned about: _____

This is a picture of a painting or sculpture I saw

THAT'S ENTERTAINMENT

BOTH MINNEAPOLIS AND ST. PAUL
consider themselves centers of culture—
and with good reason. There is so much to
see and do here, you can't possibly do it all.
Traditional African dance, Native
American flute songs, a symphony
orchestra, Broadway plays—the
entertainment possibilities are endless in
the Twin Cities.

There is no shortage of shopping
opportunities here, either. Nicollet Mall
in downtown Minneapolis marks the
center of that city's shopping district.
This is not an enclosed mall, but a street
closed off from traffic, with many stores connected by
skyways. It's also the site of the annual nighttime Holidazzle
Parades. Dayton's department store hosts a storybook, walk-
through animation show during the holiday season. See the
Calendar for more about these events.

⬆ **Visiting performers often visit Northrop Auditorium in Minneapolis.**

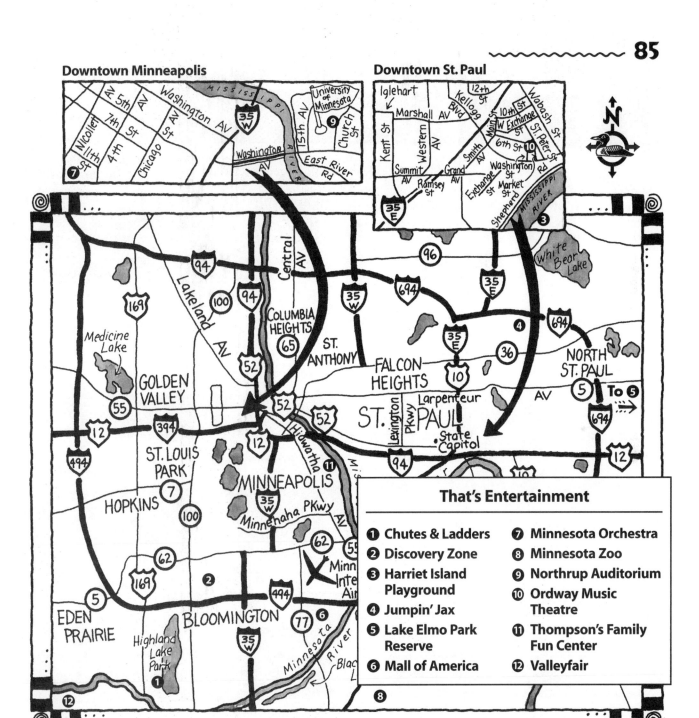

Downtown Minneapolis

Downtown St. Paul

That's Entertainment

1 **Chutes & Ladders**
2 **Discovery Zone**
3 **Harriet Island Playground**
4 **Jumpin' Jax**
5 **Lake Elmo Park Reserve**
6 **Mall of America**

7 **Minnesota Orchestra**
8 **Minnesota Zoo**
9 **Northrup Auditorium**
10 **Ordway Music Theatre**
11 **Thompson's Family Fun Center**
12 **Valleyfair**

MALL OF AMERICA

Located south of the Twin Cities, this mega-mall is constructed around an amusement park, **Knott's Camp Snoopy**. Stop in at **Lego-Land** to build things at tray tables filled with Legos. The **Nature Store** and **Bare Bones** have all kinds of fun science stuff. At **F.A.O. Schwarz**, dance on a keyboard like Tom Hanks did in the movie *Big*, or find the Barbie you can't find anywhere else. At **Oshman's Supersports U.S.A.**, you can try out the equipment before you buy it, in an indoor batting cage, basketball court, golf driving range, and more. Ready to drop? Get your feet massaged in the restrooms at **Nordstrom's**. Eat your way through more than 40 fast-food stops or relax at one of the many full-service restaurants.

The Mall of America is the largest indoor mall in the world.

An aquarium addition, the size of 35 houses, opened in the Mall of America in 1996.

⬆ **Kids having fun at Lego-Land in the Mall of America**

BUNCHES OF BEARS

How many teddy bears can you find in this toy store?
When you've circled every bear, color the scene.

AMUSEMENT PARKS

Two amusement parks lie just south of the Twin Cities. **Valleyfair**, in Shakopee, is the largest amusement park in the upper midwest. Glide down Ripple Rapids in an inner tube or scream your way through all four roller coasters. Admission includes more than 75 rides and attractions, **Whitewater Country Water Park,** and four areas especially for kids. Live stage entertainment and admission to the six-story, **Pepsi IMAX theater** are also included.

Knott's Camp Snoopy, located in the center of the Bloomington, Mall of America is the nation's largest indoor theme park. For thrills, try the **Mystery Mine Ride** or the **Paul Bunyon Log Flume.** Tuesdays are often Family Night, with one-price admission, unlimited rides, and treats for kids.

↑ **There are 75 rides at Valleyfair amusement park, including the carousel.**

Both Camp Snoopy and Valleyfair offer spectacular laser-light and fireworks shows throughout the summer.

⬸ **Located inside the Mall of America, Knott's Camp Snoopy features a high-speed roller coaster.**

WHAT'S WRONG HERE?

Circle 16 things you think are wrong with this picture.
When you're done, color the scene.

THEATER IN THE TWIN CITIES

In the early days of St. Paul, paddlewheel steamships made their way up the Mississippi each spring and summer, bringing plays and concerts. The showboat was an exciting break from the isolation early settlers often felt on this edge of the frontier. You can feel something of the pioneers' experience when you watch a show at the **Centennial Showboat,** usually docked near the Franklin Avenue Bridge. Watch the kind of shows pioneers might have seen.

⇑ **Children with the Penumbra Theatre Company dance in a recent production.**

The **Penumbra Theatre Company** offers a completely different program. Plays, musicals, and performance art pieces demonstrate the African American experience. *Black Nativity,* by Langston Hughes, mixes traditional African dance and spirituals with the Christmas Gospel story. The actors express it from an African American point of view. (These and other theaters in Minneapolis and St. Paul are listed in the Resource Guide.)

GOING TO THE THEATER

Hidden in this word search are some things you might see on a trip to the theater. Search for words vertically, horizontally, and diagonally. Can you find all 11 words? The first word has been found for you.

Word Box

actors	singing	spotlight
stage	dancing	play
curtain	scene	audience
ticket	monologue	

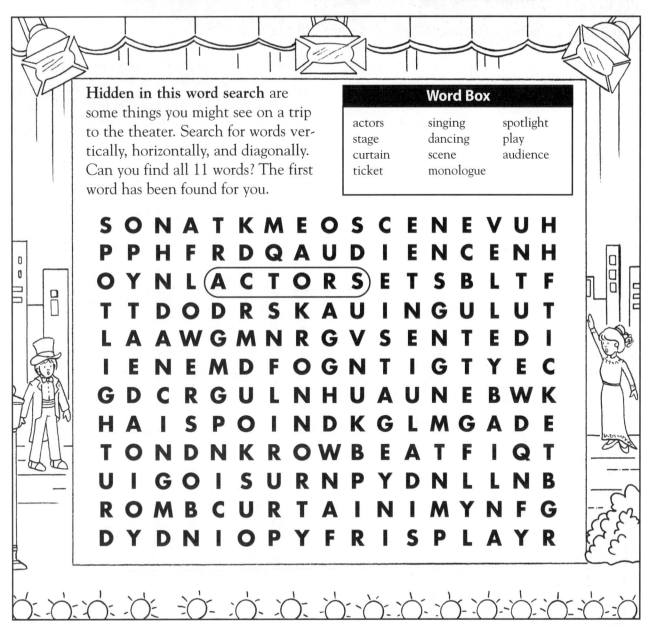

```
S O N A T K M E O S C E N E V U H
P P H F R D Q A U D I E N C E N H
O Y N L A C T O R S E T S B L T F
T T D O D R S K A U I N G U L U T
L A A W G M N R G V S E N T E D I
I E N E M D F O G N T I G T Y E C
G D C R G U L N H U A U N E B W K
H A I S P O I N D K G L M G A D E
T O N D N K R O W B E A T F I Q T
U I G O I S U R N P Y D N L L N B
R O M B C U R T A I N I M Y N F G
D Y D N I O P Y F R I S P L A Y R
```

THEATER JUST FOR KIDS

If you're not into grown-up theater and want to be entertained anyway, several theater companies in the area put on plays just for kids. The **Children's Theatre Company** is the largest professional children's theater troupe in the nation. Most plays have been taken from popular children's books. Follow the adventures of Babar or watch the Grinch steal Christmas. Another theater for kids is **Child's Play Theatre Company**. Founded in 1984, the company produces fairy tales and other children's stories. Child actors are often a part of this professional troupe. **In the Heart of the Beast Puppet and Mask Theatre** has puppets so large it often takes several people to operate just one. See the puppets at the annual May Day Festival as well as in full-length shows.

Performers at the Children's Theatre Company

All shows at Stepping Stone Theatre in the Landmark Center are performed by youth and designed for young audiences.

In the Heart of the Beast Puppet Theatre uses kids in its productions.

SCHOOL PLAY CONFUSION

Without telling anyone what you're doing, ask for a word to fill in each blank. For example, "Give me an action word." When all the blanks are filled in, read the story out loud. One of the blanks has been filled in for you.

Dana and Aaron were trying out for a _____ in the play, Peter
                                         thing

Pan. "I hope I get to be Captain _____," said Aaron. "I'd rather be
                                      thing

Tinkerbell," said Dana. "She gets to _____ through the _____
                                        action word   thing

and _____ pixie dust on everyone."
      action word

   "But Captain Hook has his own pirate _lunch box_ and can
                                              thing

make people _____ the _____," said Aaron. "He also gets
               action word   thing

chased by the _____ who _____ the _____!" said Dana.
                  animal   action word   thing

   "_____!," said Aaron. "Maybe I should try out for
      exclamation

_____ instead."
   person

Minnesota Orchestra director Eiji Oue visits with kids.
⇓

MUSIC AND DANCE

Every culture on Earth celebrates with sound and movement. How we do it varies from one group to another, but we all dance and sing and make music. You can find a wide variety of these art forms in the Twin Cities. The **Minnesota Orchestra** plays classical and popular music at its Orchestra Hall. A family music series, **Adventures in Music,** is presented September through May. The **Northrop Auditorium** presents a variety of classical, contemporary, and ethnic dance companies, touring Broadway shows and more. Its annual production of *The Nutcracker* is a Twin Cities' favorite. For two months every year, the auditorium also offers outdoor musical concerts, most of which are free. The **Ordway Music Theatre** presents outstanding theater, ethnic dance and musical groups. It's also home to the internationally famous St. Paul Chamber Orchestra.

⇑ **A performance of *The Harlem Nutcracker* at Northrop Auditorium**

WHAT'S THE DIFFERENCE?

These two scenes of a night at the symphony might look the same, but they're not. Can you find all 15 differences between the two scenes?

PLACES TO PLAY INDOORS

Older kids who are up to the challenge can enlist at **Starbase Omega**, in the Mall of America, to battle the mutant Kytef who threatens planet Previa. You will be issued regulation laser blasters and power vests. Good luck! If you still need to burn off energy, try the **Discovery Zone** or **Jumpin' Jax**. These places are as big as a department store and crammed full of climbing and jumping things to do. Depending on which one you go to, you may find a maze of tunnels and slides, a waterbed to roll on, ball pits to jump in, and rubber rooms to bounce through. Walk on a keyboard, play video games or laser tag, or step into a world of virtual reality.

If you're more into just hanging out, **Thompson's Family Fun Center** provides a friendly place to grab a snack and play video games and pinball.

↑ **Kids play at Discovery Zone.**

Several McDonald's restaurants in the area have large indoor playlands with tunnels and slides, ball pits, and free computer games.

CROSSWORD FUN

This is a crossword filled with things you can do or find at the Mall of America. Solve the crossword by figuring out the clues or completing the sentences. If you need help, use the clue box.

Across

3. You can buy souvenirs at these places.
4. Ready, ___, fire!
5. At the Mall of America, you can make music by walking on this. It's also on a piano.
6. After a quick game of laser tag you'll want a delicious _____.
7. You can play _____ games at Thompson's Family Fun Center.

Down

1. In this game of virtual _____, things look real, but they aren't!
2. You might get lost in one of these.
3. If you're old enough to save Previa, go sign up at _____ Omega.

Clue Box

reality	maze
keyboard	snack
stores	aim
video	Starbase

PLACES TO PLAY OUTDOORS

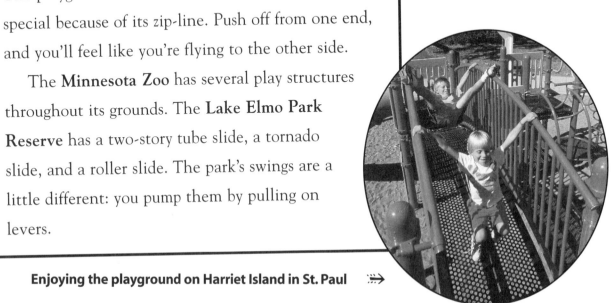

Having fun at one of the many parks in the Twin Cities

You'll find well-equipped playgrounds throughout the Twin Cities area. A few are so outstanding that they rate a special mention. **Chutes and Ladders** is a multilevel play complex with mega-tunnels and a wide variety of slides. A communication system lets you talk with friends in other sections of the complex. The playground on **Harriet Island** is special because of its zip-line. Push off from one end, and you'll feel like you're flying to the other side.

The **Minnesota Zoo** has several play structures throughout its grounds. The **Lake Elmo Park Reserve** has a two-story tube slide, a tornado slide, and a roller slide. The park's swings are a little different: you pump them by pulling on levers.

Enjoying the playground on Harriet Island in St. Paul ⇒

MY TRAVEL JOURNAL
—That's Entertainment—

These are the names of the places I visited: _____

My favorite place was: _____

What I enjoyed doing the most was: _____

The strangest thing I saw was: _____

This is a picture of something I saw • • •

8 LET'S EAT!

PERHAPS THE BEST EATING IN MINNESOTA is found not at a restaurant, but at an event—the annual state fair at the end of August. It's a great chance to sample the food of more than 300 of the Twin Cities' vendors. But if you're not in town at fair time, don't despair, there's sure to be a restaurant in Minneapolis or St. Paul to suit your family's tastes. The choices range from the French cuisine of Forepaugh's to an A&W Drive-In. If you're really up for a taste of Minnesota, look for cheese curds or Walleye on a stick. Chow down at some of the great places for kids described in this chapter.

⇑ **A sunny day at the Farmers Market**

Even though it's indoors, the Rain Forest Café looks like a jungle. ⇢

Let's Eat!

1. Bridgeman's
2. Broadway Pizza
3. The Carousel
4. Circus Pizza
5. Cosetta's
6. Fuddruckers
7. Heartthrob Café
8. It's Greek to Me
9. Kahn's Mongolian Barbeque
10. Malt Shop
11. Rain Forest Café

PERFECT PIZZA

Broadway Pizza has won many awards for the best pizza in the Twin Cities. Broadway is famous for its sausage pie, but the white pizza is delicious, too. It is loaded with chunks of chicken, fresh tomatoes, and lots of gooey cheese. The Broadway Pizza on West River Road has two train cars you can dine in and toy trains everywhere.

You'll find several **Circus Pizza** restaurants in the metro area. Circus Pizza is a video arcade and play zone with a restaurant in the middle. The Circus Pizza in the town of Edina just southwest of Minneapolis has the largest climb and slide. Another Circus Pizza in Brooklyn Park northwest of Minneapolis has bumper cars and a merry-go-round.

⬆ **Broadway Pizza is a popular restaurant.**

Ancient Romans thought tomatoes were poisonous. When Romans ate pizza for breakfast, they often put leeks, onions, fish, and cheese on it—but no tomato sauce.

PLACE THE PIZZA

Find the slice of pizza on the left that matches the pizza on the right. Then draw a line connecting each slice with its pizza.

BEST ETHNIC EATS

At **Kahn's Mongolian Barbeque**, kids pay based on their height. Select your favorite meats and veggies (so you don't have to eat anything you don't like!), then watch the chefs barbecue it on a sizzling Mongolian grill. If you tip the chef, you can ring the gong.

If you like Italian food, try **Cosetta's** in St. Paul for delicious homemade pastas, pizzas, and authentic Italian-baked dishes like lasagna and veal parmesan. Upstairs, the rooms are decorated with pictures of historic St. Paul. Many are of Little Italy, which no longer exists because of frequent flooding.

Maybe you'd prefer **It's Greek to Me**, located in Minneapolis. For something different, try saganaki—a flaming cheese appetizer—or stuffed grape leaves with either beef or vegetable filling. The portions are large, but try to leave room for baklava (bahk-lah-vah)—a flaky, honey-sweet dessert that will melt on your tongue.

If you're in town on Labor Day weekend, here's your chance to go to an authentic Native American pow-wow. Join in the All Nations dance and try some fry bread, served hot.

HIDE AND SEEK!

Hidden in this picture are different kinds of food that can be found in Minneapolis and St. Paul. See if you can find at least 12 foods. If you need help, use the clue box.

WEIRD RESTAURANTS

The **Heartthrob Café and Philadelphia Bandstand** are located across the street from the Minnesota Children's Museum and a block south of the Science Museum. Servers glide around the restaurant on roller skates. The specialty is crispy, spicy French fries.

At the **Rain Forest Café**, in the Mall of America, sounds of tropical birds fill the trees overhead. In the distance, an elephant trumpets. Wall-size aquariums of exotic fish divide sections of the room. Thundershowers, followed by a rainbow, occur several times every hour. The food here is delicious and plentiful.

⬆ **Watch for rain at the Rain Forest Café.**

Heartthrob Café features 1950s-style dining. ⇢

WHAT'S THE DIFFERENCE?

These two restaurant scenes might look the same, but they aren't.
Find and circle all 15 differences between the two scenes.

BEST BITES

Best Burger:

At **Fuddruckers**, you can construct your own burger masterpiece using items from the fixings bar. Kids under 12 eat free week-nights after 4:30.

Best Malts and Shakes:

The **Malt Shop** makes them the old-fashioned way—with real ice cream. They offer 25 single flavors but the combos are unlimited. Their kids' menu offers a great variety of choices—you can even get fruit instead of fries.

Best Ice Cream Sundae:

Bridgeman's is known for great ice-cream treats. Plan your dessert first. Then, order your meal based on how much stomach space you'll need for that particular dessert.

Best View:

Ask for seating on **The Carousel** restaurant when you dine on the 22nd floor of the Radisson Hotel in St. Paul. The restaurant rotates! In about 45 minutes, you can see the Mississippi and all of St. Paul.

⬆ **The Carousel Restaurant rotates as diners eat their meals.**

The annual Taste of Minnesota is held on the 4th of July weekend at the Capitol grounds. Here, restaurants from the Twin Cities area offer their specialties at bite-size prices.

MY TRAVEL JOURNAL
—Let's Eat!—

These are the names of some restaurants I ate at:

_____

My favorite restaurant was: _____

The food I enjoyed there the most was: _____

The most unusual food I ate was: _____

Mt least favorite food was: _____

This is a picture of a restaurant I visited

CALENDAR OF EVENTS IN THE TWIN CITIES

Please call or write to be sure of details of events. Although every effort has been made to provide accurate information, days, times, and admission fees may change.

January

St. Paul Winter Carnival

St. Paul Winter Carnival Association, 339 Bremer Building, St. Paul, 55101. (612) 223-4710. The carnival includes parades, treasure hunt, ice sculptures in Rice Park, the Children's Pepsi Playground on the Capital Mall, winter sports competitions, and lots of silliness. Held from the fourth weekend in January to the first Sunday in February.

⇒ Kids play at the St. Paul Winter Carnival

Grand Day Parade honoring King Boreas

Held on the first Saturday of the month, it's followed by a torchlight parade the next Saturday. Most events are either free or require a $3 Winter Carnival Button, available at local grocery and convenience stores. A few events charge additional fees. Watch the Pioneer Press for details on events and locations as well as treasure-hunt clues.

February

Kidfest

St. Paul Civic Center, 143 West Fourth Street, St. Paul 55401. (612) 224-7361 or (612) 566-5108. Children's activities, 2 entertainment stages, free kiddie midway, play areas, petting zoo, sing-alongs, games of chance, and lots of fun. Adults $6, kids ages 1 to 12, $2. Children under age 1 are admitted free. Held the last weekend in February. Saturday 10:00 a.m. to 8:00 p.m. and Sunday noon to 6:00 p.m.

March

St. Patrick's Day parades

Held at noon in both cities. For $5, anyone can walk in the St. Paul parade, as long as they are wearing green. Information (St. Paul): 24 East 4th Street, St. Paul, MN 55101. (612) 298-1950. Parade starts at noon and lasts approximately 1 hour. Check local papers for parade route.

Osman Temple Shrine Circus
St. Paul Civic Center Arena, late March or early April. For information, contact: Bob Janecek, 2750 Sibley Memorial Highway, St. Paul, MN 55121. (612) 452-5660 or (800) 824-7287. Ticket prices range from $3 to $20, depending on seating choice. Children under 2 are admitted free.

Dayton's/Bachman's Flower Show
In the 8th floor auditorium of Dayton's Department Store, 700 Nicollet Mall, Minneapolis, MN 55402. (612) 375-2200. A walk-through display of flowers in a parklike setting. Free.

April

Minnesota Horse Expo
Held at the Minnesota State Fairgrounds, St. Paul, MN 55108. 922-8666. A don't miss event for horse lovers. More than 30 breeds are represented, with 300 exhibitor booths providing all kinds of horse information and products. Admission for adults is $5; age 65 and over, $4; children 6 to 12, $2; children under 5, free.

Festival of Nations
St. Paul Civic Center, 1694 Como Avenue, St. Paul, MN 55108. (612) 222-6347 or (612) 647-0191. Held in late April or early May. This is a multicultural extravaganza featuring displays of customs, cultures, crafts, ethnic foods, folk costumes and dance, music, storytelling and more. Continuous performances by 75 different folk dance groups. More than 50 different ethnic groups represented. Admission: Adults $6 in advance or $8 at the door; children 5 to 16, $4; children under 5, free.

May

Scottish Country Fair
Macalester College, 1600 Grand Avenue, St. Paul, MN 55105. (612) 696-6239. Open from 10:00 a.m. to 6:00 p.m. on the first Saturday of May. This fair features highland dancing, a bagpipe competition, shepherding, games of strength, a juried art fair, food, living history demonstrations, and more. Admission is $6 for adults, $3.50 for seniors and children ages 6 to 12. Children under 6 are admitted free.

Cinco De Mayo Mexican Fiesta
On the west side of St. Paul. Celebrates the 1862 Mexican victory over the French. Parade, Mexican food, and entertainment. Most events are free. See local newspapers for times and locations. For information, contact: 176 Concord Street, St. Paul, MN 55107. (612) 222-6347.

Syttende Mai
Held on May 17th, Norwegian Constitution Day. Parade in downtown Minneapolis on the Saturday closest to the 17th, with floats, bands, Norwegian crafts, foods, etc., throughout downtown Minneapolis. For more information, contact: The Sons of Norway, 1455 West Lake Street, Minneapolis, MN 55408. (612) 827-3611.

May Day Parade and Festival

At Powderhorn Park. Held on the first Sunday in May, produced by In the Heart of the Beast Puppet Theatre, this is a very popular event for children and families. Local bands and street performers. For information, contact: In the Heart of the Beast Puppet and Mask Theatre, 1500 East Lake Street, Minneapolis, MN 55440. Free.

⬆ **The Heart of the Beast performs.**

Twin Cities Juneteenth Celebration

At 1701 Oak Park Avenue North, Minneapolis, MN 55411. (612) 377-7000. The largest African American celebration in Minnesota. Always on the Saturday closest to June 16th. Most events are free.

June

Danish Day

Celebrated on the first Sunday in June. Times and locations vary from year to year. The celebration includes folk dancing and Danish food and games. Admission: about $2. For more information, contact: The Danish American Center, 4200 Cedar Avenue, Minneapolis, MN 55407. (612) 729-3800.

Volksfest Day (German Day)

Volksfest Association of Minnesota, 301 Summit Avenue, St. Paul, MN 55102. (612) 222-7027. Held on the second Sunday in June, from 11:00 a.m. to 6:00 p.m., on the Volksfest Association grounds. Includes folk dancing, German foods, and a variety of other events. Free.

Midsommar

At American Swedish Institute, 2600 Park Avenue, Minneapolis, MN 55110. (612) 871-4907. Traditional Swedish holiday celebrating the day when sunlight conquers the long winter darkness. Music, folk dancing, crafts, and food. Held on the third Saturday in June, 10:00 a.m. to 4:00 p.m. Most events are free.

Svenskarnes Day (Swedish Day)

Held in Minnehaha Park on the fourth Sunday of June. This event includes dancing, music, and Swedish food. For information, contact: The American Swedish Institute, 2600 Park Avenue, Minneapolis, MN 55110. (612) 871-4907.

Bavarian Sommerfest

At Gasthaus Bavarian Hunter, 3 miles north of Highway 36 on County Road 15 at 64, Stillwater, MN 55988. (612) 439-7128. Held on the last weekend of June. Sunday is Family Day. Admission is $1.

July

Taste of Minnesota

At State Capital Grounds, Aurora and Constitution Avenues, St. Paul, MN 55105. (612) 228-0018. July 4th weekend celebration. Food, food, food, live entertainment, and fireworks. Admission is free, but you must purchase food tickets.

Norway Day

At Minnehaha Park, second Sunday in July. Includes a children's flag parade, Norwegian music, folk dancing, and ethnic foods. For information, contact: The Sons of Norway, 1455 West Lake Street, Minneapolis, MN 55408. (612) 827-3611.

Aquatennial

Begins the third week in July. Ten days, 2 parades, plus sand-castle sculptures at Lake Calhoun and an annual milk-carton boat race on Lake Calhoun. Water skiing on Lake of the Isles and Formula 1 racing on the Mississippi. For more information, contact: The Aquatennial Association, 43 SE Main Street, Minneapolis, MN 55414. (612) 331-8371.

Rondo Days Parade and Festival

At Martin Luther King Center, 270 North Kent Street, St. Paul, MN 55102. (612) 646-6597. Celebrates the history of the African American Rondo community with music, storytelling, children's entertainment, and more. Held on the third Saturday in July, 10:00 a.m. to 10:00 p.m.

Fourth of July fireworks

In St. Paul, you'll find them at the Taste of Minnesota on the Capital grounds. In Minneapolis, you'll find them along the riverfront at historic St. Anthony Main. At the Mall of America, see the indoor fireworks and laser light and water show.

August

Confederate Air Force Aircraft Show

Holman Field, St. Paul Downtown Airport, St. Paul, MN 55107. Usually held on the first weekend in August but can be in July or later in August. $7 for adults, $5 for seniors, $3 for children ages 3 to 12. Children under age 3 are admitted free. Group rates for scout troops and reduced rates for low-income families available. Bus groups encouraged to come on the opening Friday of the event. For information, contact: John Schuck, Public Relations, 310 Airport Road, Fleming Field, South St. Paul, MN 55075. (612) 347-1750.

Ukranian Day

Celebrated in Minnehaha Park on the Sunday following August 24th. Features singing, folk dancing, and displays of Ukranian eggs and embroidery. For more information, contact: Luba Mensheha, 509 7th Avenue NE, Minneapolis, MN 55413. (612) 379-8434.

⬆ **Visitors at the Minnesota State Fair**

Minnesota State Fair

At State Fair Grounds, 1265 Snelling Avenue South, St. Paul, MN 55108. (612) 642-2200. One of the largest state fairs in the nation. This 12-day fair starts in the last week of August and ends on Labor Day. Rides, food, exhibits, children's barn, etc. Two days are designated as Children's Days, when children under 18 are admitted for $1. Admission is $5 for adults, $3 if purchased in advance. $4 for seniors over 65, $3 if purchased in advance. $4 for children 5 to 15. Children under 5 are free.

Renaissance Festival

At 1244 Canterbury Road, Suite 306, Shakopee, MN 55379. (612) 445-7461. Weekends and Labor Day from mid-August through late September, 9:00 a.m. to 7:00 p.m. Reenactment of a renaissance-era harvest festival. Adult admission, $13.95, children ages 5 to 12, $4.95. Free for children under 5.

Airport Days

At Minneapolis-St. Paul International Airport, third weekend in August, 9:00 a.m. to 5:00 p.m.

Behind the scenes tours; exhibits and airplanes are on display. Free. Metropolitan Airports Commission, Public Affairs, (612) 726-8172.

September

Powwow

Held at Fort Snelling State Park on Labor Day Weekend. Native American dance and drum group competitions, food, and fun. Admission to all events, all weekend is $7 for ages 6 and over. Senior citizens and under 7 are admitted free. For information, call (612) 724-3129.

Oktoberfest

At Gasthaus Bavarian Hunter, 3 miles north of Highway 36 on County Road 15 at 64, Stillwater, MN 55988. (612) 439-7128. Usually held in late September. Sunday is Family Day. Admission is $1.

Fall Colors Art Festival

Downtown in Lowell Park, Stillwater, MN 55988. (612) 439-7700. Arts, food, and music. Free.

October

Zoo Boo at Como Zoo

At Como Zoological Society, 1250 Kaufman Drive, St. Paul, MN 55103. (612) 487-1485. A non-scary alternative to trick-or-treating for children under 10. Children walk through a decorated pathway and collect treats at various stations throughout the zoo grounds attended by costumed characters. It is held on the two weekends before Halloween, Friday to Sunday, about 5:30 to 8:00 p.m. Call in October for exact days and times.

Halloween Haunted Happenings

At the Minnesota Zoo, 12101 Johnny Cake Ridge Road, Apple Valley, MN 55124. Includes hayrides, trick-or-treating, and a haunted house. Usually on the 2 weekends before Halloween, from 9:00 a.m. to 8:00 p.m., but may vary. Call the Zoo-to-Do hotline in October: (612) 432-9000. Admission is $4 for children 3 to 12, $8 for age 13 to adult, $5 for seniors, free for children under 3.

November

Dayton's Holiday Show

In the 8th floor auditorium, 700 Nicollet Mall, Minneapolis, MN 55402. (612) 375-2200. Almost life-size moving figures act out a classic children's story in a series of scenes that you can walk through. Admission is free.

Holidazzle Parade

Every night at 6:30 p.m., from the Friday after Thanksgiving to December 30th, Nicollet Mall, downtown Minneapolis. A spectacular ½-hour event in which storybook characters come to life in song and costumes made of millions of tiny lights. For further information, call the Minneapolis Downtown Council, (612) 338-3807. Free.

December

Hill House Holidays

At the James J. Hill House, 240 Summit Avenue, St. Paul, MN 55102. (612) 297-2555. The busy day of a holiday party is reenacted by the Hill family servants, and tour participants become part of the drama. This special program runs the week before Christmas through New Year's Eve. Call for admission prices.

3M Club Christmas Show

Held at the Bethel College Great Hall, 3900 Bethel Drive, Arden Hills, MN 55112. The 3M Symphony and women's and men's choruses perform traditional Christmas music. Two shows, at 2:00 and 7:00 p.m. $8 general admission. Tickets available in advance through 3M Club office, (612) 773-6079.

A Victorian Christmas

Held indoors at various locations in the Twin Cities. Features seasonal food and drink. Characters, such as Father Christmas, are costumed in Victorian attire. Admission price, dates, and times vary from year to year. Generally held on weekends from Thanksgiving until Christmas. For more information, contact: The Minnesota Renaissance Festival, 1244 Canterbury Road, Suite 306, Shakopee, MN 55379. (612) 445-7361.

RESOURCE GUIDE: WHEN, WHAT, AND HOW MUCH?

Although all of the sights listed in this guide offer programs for children and families, not all programs offered by these places are suitable. Before attending a theater production, it is a good idea to have your parents check to see if the program offered at that time is OK for you to see.

The information contained in this resource guide changes often. Call before you plan your trip for current days and hours of operation as well as admissions.

If You Get Lost

Do you know what to do if you get lost? Make a plan with your parents about what to do if you lose them. If you forget what to do and you're in a store, go to a person working at a cash register. If you are outside, look for a mother with children. Tell her you're lost.

If there is an emergency and you need the police, fire department, or an ambulance, you can dial 911 from any phone. You won't need coins.

Important Numbers

AAA Minnesota, 24-hour emergency road service. In St. Paul and east suburbs, plus Carver, Scott, Dakota, Washington, and Anoka Counties, (612) 891-8000. In Minneapolis and west suburbs and Hennepin County, (612) 927-2727. Auto travel routings, (612) 891-8200.

The Connection, community events bulletin board, (612) 922-9000

Emergencies, for Police, Fire, and Paramedics, call 911

Greater Minneapolis Convention and Visitors Association, 1219 Marquette Avenue, Minneapolis. (612) 348-4313 or (800) 445-7412

Metro Connections Bus Tours, 1219 Marquette Avenue, Suite 110, Minneapolis, 55403. Three-hour bus tours with guides. Pick-up points in downtown Minneapolis, downtown St. Paul, and the Mall of America. Admission is $18 for adults, $10 for kids. (612) 333-8687 or (800) 747-8687

Minneapolis City Hall, 350 South 5th Street, Minneapolis, 55415. Open Monday to Friday from 8:00 to 4:30. Admission is free. (612) 673-3000

Minneapolis Parks and Recreation, 200 Grain Exchange Building, 400 S. Fourth Street, Minneapolis, 55415-1400. (612) 661-4800

Minneapolis RiverCity Trolley, 125 S.E. Main Street, Minneapolis, 55414. Open Monday through Sunday from Convent Center and St. Anthony Main. One-hour rides are available every 20 minutes. For trolley information, call (612) 661-4700. $2 for children ages 2–12; $4 for adults.

St. Paul Calendar of Events, 55 E. Fifth Street, Suite 101, St. Paul, 55101. (612) 297-6985

St. Paul City Hall, near St. Peter Street, Fourth Street, Wabasha Street, and Kellogg Boulevard at 15 West Kellogg Boulevard, St. Paul, 55102. (612) 266-8989

St. Paul Convention and Visitors Bureau, 445 Minnesota Street, St. Paul, 55101. Information booths at State Capital, Landmark Center, Science Museum, and City Hall. (612) 297-6985 or (800) 627-6101

St. Paul Division of Parks and Recreation, 300 City Hall Annex, 25 West Fourth Street, St. Paul, 55102. (612) 292-6548

TicketMaster, (612) 989-5151

Tourism Hotlines, Minneapolis, (612) 370-9103; St. Paul, (612) 222-1000

Twin Cities Tourism Attractions Association of Minnesota, 1550 East 79th St., Bloomington, 55425. (612) 858-8493

Weather, (612) 375-0830

What They Cost and When They're Open

All Seasons Golf Dome, 7552 South West Point Douglas Road, Cottage Grove, 55016. Open daily from 8:00 a.m. to 9:00 p.m. Admission is $5.75. (612) 459-2135

American Swedish Institute, 2600 Park Avenue, Minneapolis, 55110. Open Tuesday, Thursday, Friday, Saturday, noon to 4:00 p.m.; Wednesday, noon to 8:00 p.m.; Sunday, 1:00 to 5:00 p.m. Closed Monday and holidays. Admission is $3 for adults, $2 for kids ages 6 to 18. Children under age 6 are admitted free. Free to all visitors on the first Wednesday of every month. (612) 871-4907

Bandana Square, 1021 Bandana Boulevard East, St. Paul, 55108. (612) 642-1509

Bell Museum of Natural History, University of Minnesota, 10 Church Street S.E. Minneapolis, 55455. Open Tuesday to Friday from 9:00 a.m. to 5:00 p.m.; Saturday, 10:00 a.m. to 5:00 p.m.; Sunday, noon to 5:00 p.m. Closed on Monday. Admission is $3 for adults; $2 for children ages 3 to 16. No charge for admission on Thursday. Information and registrations (612) 624-7083; wildlife information (612) 624-1374

Bloomington Ice Garden, 3600 West 98th Street, Bloomington, 55431. Call ahead for open skating and open hockey times. Admission is $2.50 for adults and $2 for kids age 17 and younger. Skate rental is $1.50. (612) 948-8842

⬆ **Boom Island**

Boom Island, Central Mississippi Riverfront Regional Park near Minneapolis. Free parking lot is on Sibley Street N.E. at the east end of the Plymouth Avenue Bridge (N.E. 8th Avenue).

Broadway Pizza:
— 2025 North West River Road, Minneapolis, 55411. (612) 529-7745
— 2512 Kenzie Trail, St. Anthony, 55418. (612) 789-5562

Café Latte, 850 Grand Avenue, St. Paul, 55105. (612) 224-5687

Cafesjian's Carousel, 445 Minnesota Street, St. Paul, 55101. Located in St. Paul's Town Square. Open Friday through Sunday from 10:00 a.m. to 5:00 p.m. Admission is $1. (612) 290-2774

Capital City Trolley, look for green and red Capital City Trolley signs throughout St. Paul. Open Monday through Sunday from 11:00 a.m. to 5:00 p.m. Admission is 25 cents per ride. For route maps and information, call (800) 566-2720 or (612) 223-5600.

The Carousel Restaurant, Radisson Hotel, 11 East Kellogg Blvd., St. Paul, 55101. (612) 292-0408

Cathedral of St. Paul, 239 Selby Avenue, St. Paul, 55102. Open daily from 7:30 a.m. to 6:00 p.m. Guided tours on Monday, Wednesday and Friday at 1:00 p.m. Admission is free, but donations are accepted. (612) 228-1766

Centennial Showboat, usually moored near the East River Flats under the Franklin Avenue Bridge. Check with the ticket office before heading to your performance. (612) 624-2345 or (612) 625-4001

Central Mississippi Riverfront Regional Park, along both banks of the Mississippi River in Minneapolis from Plymouth Avenue to the I-35 West Bridge. For information, contact the Minneapolis Park and Recreation Board. Open from sunrise to sunset year round. Admission is free.

Child's Play Theatre Company, 1001 Highway 7, Hopkins. Show times and locations vary. Admission is $8 for adults, $6 for kids ages two and over. Children under two admitted free. Call ahead for a complete schedule (612) 925-5250.

Children's Theatre Company, Minneapolis Institute of Art, 2400 Third Avenue South, Minneapolis. Performances on Tuesday through Saturday at 7:30 p.m. Saturday at 11:00 a.m. and

2:00 p.m.; Sunday at 2:00 p.m. and 5:00 p.m. Admission ranges from $9.50 to $24. (612) 874-0400

Chutes and Ladders, Hyland Lake Park Preserve, 10145 East Bush Lake Road, Bloomington, 55438. Park is open year round. Playground is open as weather permits. Admission is $4 daily parking fee or $20 annual Hennepin Parks Permit. Call the Visitor Center (612) 941-4362 or the Nature Center (612) 941-7993

Circus Pizza:
— 8943 University Avenue N.E., Blaine, 55434. (612) 780-5334
— 7577 Brooklyn Boulevard, Brooklyn Park, 55443. (612) 560-4422
— 4336 Burnhaven Drive, Burnsville, 55337. (612) 435-3095
— 7505 France Avenue South, Edina, 55435. (612) 831-4077
— 4411 Winnetka Avenue North, New Hope, 55428. (612) 533-2282
— 1422 S. Robert Street, St. Paul, 55118. (612) 455-4247

Como Park Zoo and Conservatory, between Hamline and Lexington Avenues on Midway Parkway and Kaufman Drive. Como Pool is located at Horton Ave. and N. Lexington Parkway, St. Paul. The playground is located in the picnic area on Beulah Lane near the intersection of Horton Avenue. Open from April 1 to September 30, 8:00 a.m. to 8:00 p.m.; October 1 to March 31, 8:00 a.m. to 5:00 p.m. (612) 487-1485

Cosetta's Italian Market & Pizzeria, 211 West Seventh Street, St. Paul, 55102. (612) 222-3476

Edinborough Park, 7700 York Ave., South, Edina, 55435. Open Sunday through Thursday from 9:00 a.m. to 9:00 p.m.; Friday and Saturday, 9:00 a.m. to 5:00 p.m. Special children's activities scheduled Tuesdays and Thursdays at noon. Daily pass is $3, skate rental $1.50. (612) 893-9890

Eloise Butler Wildflower Garden and Bird Sanctuary, Theodore Wirth Parkway and Glenwood Avenue, Minneapolis, 55415. Open daily from April 1 to October 31, 8:00 a.m until dark. Admission is free. (612) 348-5702

F. Scott Fitzgerald Theatre, 10 East Exchange, St. Paul, 55101. Located on the corner of Exchange and Wabasha. Hours and admission vary according to performance. (612) 290-1200

Father Hennepin Bluff Park, corner of Main and Fifth Street S.E. in Minneapolis; connected to Nicollet Island Park by Historic Main Street.

Forepaugh's, 276 S. Exchange St., St. Paul, 55102. (612) 224-5606

Fort Snelling Historic Site, Minnesota Highways Five and 55, St. Paul, between the Twin Cities International Airport and the Mississippi River. Open from May 1 to October 31, Monday to Saturday, 10:00 a.m. to 5:00 p.m.; Sunday, noon to 5:00 p.m. Admission is $4 for adults, $2 for children ages 6 to 15; children under age 5 are free. (612) 726-1171 or (612) 725-2413.

Fort Snelling State Park, 6000 Minnehaha Avenue, St. Paul, 55155. Open year round from 8:00 a.m. to 10:00 p.m. Admission is $4 for two consecutive days or $18 for a one calendar year. Permit is good at all Minnesota state parks. (612) 726-9247

Foshay Tower, 821 Marquette Avenue, Minneapolis, 55402. Open Monday to Friday from noon to 4:00 p.m.; Saturday, 11:00 a.m. to 3:00 p.m. Closed during the winter and on Sundays. Admission is $3 for adults, $2 for children and seniors. (612) 341-2522

Fuddruckers:
— 3801 Minnesota Drive, Bloomington, 55435. (612) 835-3833
— 2740 Snelling Avenue, Roseville, 55113. (612) 636-3833
— 6445 Wayzata Boulevard, St. Louis Park, 55426. (612) 593-3833
— 1435 Nicollet Court, Burnsville, 55337. (612) 435-5733

Gervais Lake, access from Keller Parkway just north of Arcade Street intersection. Contact St. Paul Parks and Recreation for more information.

Gibbs Farm Museum, 2097 Larpenteur Avenue, Falcon Heights, 55113. Open from May to October, Tuesday through Friday, 10:00 a.m. to 4:00 p.m.; Saturday and Sunday, noon to 4:00 p.m. Admission is $2.50 for adults, $1 for children. (612) 646-8629

Golf Mountain, third floor, 376 North Garden, Mall of America, Bloomington, 55425. Open from Monday to Thursday, 10:00 a.m. to 9:30 p.m.; Friday to Saturday, 10:00 a.m. to 10:00 p.m.; Sunday, 11 a.m. to 7:00 p.m. Admission is $5 for adults, $4 for children ages 4 and under. (612) 883-8899

Grand Slam Sports, Highway 13 and Cedar (Highway 77), Eagan, 55122. Features mini golf, batting cages, arcade, play zone, basketball court and laser tag. Hours: Sunday to Thursday; 10:00 a.m. to 10:00 p.m. Friday to Saturday; 10:00 a.m. to midnight Admission is $5 and up. (612) 452-6485

⬆ **Kevin Garnett goes for two points.**

Harriet Island, follow the signs from the Wabasha Street Bridge. The playground is on the north side of the island. Open year round. Admission is free.

Heartthrob Café and Philadelphia Bandstand, 30 East Eighth Street, St. Paul, 55101. (612) 224-2783

Hubert H. Humphrey Metrodome, 501 Chicago Avenue South, Minneapolis, 55415. Admission varies. (612) 375-7444 or (612) 375-1116

IDS Building, 80 S. Eighth Street, Minneapolis, 55440. (612) 671-3131

In the Heart of the Beast Puppet and Mask Theatre, 1500 East Lake Street, Minneapolis, 55407. Hours vary. Tickets are usually $5 to $8. (612) 721-2535

Indian Mounds Park, in St. Paul on the east bank of the Mississippi on both sides of Mounds Boulevard.

Inside Sports Training Center and Batting Cages, 1550 Rice Street, St. Paul, 55117. Open year round, 7 days a week. Hours and admission vary. (612) 489-5019

It's Greek to Me, on the corner of Lake and Lyndale at 626 West Lake Street, Minneapolis, 55408. (612) 825-9922

James J. Hill House, 240 Summit Avenue, St. Paul, 55102. Open Wednesday to Saturday from 10:00 a.m. to 3:30 p.m. Admission is $4 for adults and $2 for children ages 6 to 15. Free for children under age 5. (612) 297-2555

Jumpin' Jax, 3001 White Bear Avenue, Maplewood, 55109. Open Monday to Thursday from 9:00 a.m. to 9:00 p.m.; Friday and Saturday, 9:00 a.m. to 10:00 p.m.; Sunday 10:00 a.m. to 8:00 p.m. Admission is $6. Parents accompanied by kids are admitted free. (612) 770-9860

Kahn's Mongolian Barbecue, 2720 Snelling Avenue, Roseville, 55113. (612) 631-3398

Keller Regional Park, extends from the north end of Kohlman Lake to the south end of Lake Phalen in Saint Paul.

Knott's Camp Snoopy, Mall of America, 5000 Center Court, Bloomington, 55425-5500. Open Monday to Friday from 10:00 a.m. to 9:30 p.m.; Saturday, 9:30 a.m.. to 9:30 p.m.; Sunday, 10:00 a.m. to 7:00 p.m. Admission varies. (612) 883-8600

Lake Calhoun, located at 3000 East Calhoun Parkway, Minneapolis. Open year round. Admission is free. (612) 348-5364

Lake Elmo Park Preserve, on Highway 19 and 10th Street North in Lake Elmo. Hours vary according to season. Admission is $3 daily or $14 for an annual pass. (612) 731-3851

Lake Harriet, at 4740 East Lake Parkway and Minneapolis Parkway, Minneapolis, 55406. Open year round. Admission is free. (612) 661-4800

Lake of the Isles, on Lake of the Isles Parkway at both West 27th and West 28th Streets, Minneapolis. Open year round. Admission is free.

Landmark Center, 75 West Fifth Street, St. Paul, 55102. Open Monday to Friday from 9:00 to 5:00. Tours available Thursday at 11:00 a.m. and Sunday at 1:00 p.m. Admission is free. (612) 292-3230

Lava Links, West County Road B-2, Roseville, 55113. Open Monday through Thursday from 10:00 a.m. to 10:00 p.m. Admission is $4.25 for adults and $3.75 for kids ages 11 to 16; $3.25 for kids age 10 and under. (612) 628-9956

Mall of America, 60 East Broadway, Bloomington, 55425. Open Monday to Saturday from 10:00 a.m. to 9:30 p.m.; Sunday, 11:00 a.m. to 7:00 p.m. (612) 883-8800

The Malt Shop
— Snelling Avenue at I-94, St. Paul, 55105. (612) 645-4643
— 50th Street at Bryant Avenue South, St. Paul, 55419. (612) 824-1352

Minneapolis Chain of Lakes Regional Park, from Lake Harriet and to Lake of the Isles. Hours vary. Open year round. Admission is free.

Minneapolis Planetarium, 300 Nicollet Mall, Minneapolis, 55401. Hours vary. Admission is $4 for kids ages 13 and older, $2.50 for kids ages 12 and younger. Children less than 2 are admitted free. (612) 372-6644

Minneapolis RiverCity Trolley, 125 S.E. Main Street, Minneapolis, 55414. Open Monday through Sunday from Convent Center and St. Anthony Main. One-hour rides are available every 20 minutes. For trolley information, call (612) 661-4700. Cost for an all-day pass: $2 for children ages 2–12; $4 for adults.

Minnehaha Regional Park, off Minnehaha Avenue and Godfrey Road. Hours vary seasonally. Open year round. Admission is free.

Minnesota Arctic Blast, (hockey team), 3800 First Bank Place, P.O. 357, Minneapolis, 55440-0357. Season runs from June to August. Call for schedule. Admission ranges from $7 to $13. (612) 376-7825

Minnesota Air Guard Museum, at the intersection of Highway 55 and Highway 62 at the Air Force Base. Tell the guard at the gate that you are there to tour the Air Guard Museum and he will give you directions. Open from April 15th to September 15. Open weekends 11:00 a.m. to 4:00 p.m. and by appointment. Admission is $2 for adults age 16 and older and $1 for children. (612) 725-5609

Minnesota Children's Museum, on the corner of Seventh and Wabasha Streets at 10 West. Seventh Street, St. Paul, 55102. Open Monday to Sunday from 9:00 a.m. to 5:00 p.m.; Thursday, 9:00 a.m. to 8:00 p.m. Admission is $5.95 for ages 3 to 60. Under age 2 and over 60 is $3.95. (612) 644-5305

Minnesota History Center, 345 Kellogg Blvd., St. Paul, 55102. Open Tuesday, Wednesday, Friday, and Saturday from 11:00 a.m. to 4:00 p.m.; Thursday, 11:00 a.m. to 7:30 p.m.; Sunday, 1:00 to 5:00 p.m. Admission is $2. (612) 296-6126

Minnesota Orchestra, 1111 Nicollet Mall, Minneapolis, 55403. Presents classical and popular music programs. Special children's programs are sometimes held. Hours and admission vary. (612) 371-5656

Minnesota State Capitol Building, Aurora and Constitution Avenues, St. Paul, 55155. Open weekdays from 8:30 a.m. to 5:00 p.m.; Saturday, 10:00 a.m. to 4:00 p.m.; Sunday, 1:00 to 4:00 p.m. Admission is free. (612) 297-3521

Minnesota State Fair, 1265 Snelling Avenue North, St. Paul, 55108. Open from 6:00 a.m. to midnight. Admission is $5 for adults, $4 for kids ages 5 to 12. Children age 5 and younger are free. (612) 296-2881

Minnesota Thunder Soccer, 4801 West 81st Street, Bloomington, 55437. Season runs from April to Labor Day. Most matches are held on Saturdays at 7:30 p.m. Admission is $11 for premium reserved seats, $8 for adults, and $5 for kids under age 19. (612) 893-1442

Minnesota Timberwolves Basketball, Season runs November to April. Admission ranges from $10 to $46. For tickets call (612) 337-3865 or TicketMaster.

Minnesota Twins Baseball, H.H.H. Metrodome. There are 81 home games in the season, which runs from April to September. Admission is $4 to $12. (612) 338-9467

Minnesota Valley National Wildlife Refuge, 3815 East 80th Street, Bloomington, 55425. Open from April to December 31 at 9:00 a.m. to 9:00 p.m., not including Sunday and Monday. Open from January 1 to March 31, excluding Monday, Wednesday, and Thursday. Admission is free. (612) 335-2299

Minnesota Vikings Football, there are ten home games in the season, which runs from August to December. Admission is $20 to $45. tickets and information, call (612) 338-8828.

⬆ **Tigers at the Minnesota Zoo.**

The Minnesota Zoo, 12101 Johnny Cake Ridge Road, Apple Valley, 55124. Open from Memorial Day weekend to Labor Day, Monday to Saturday, 9:00 a.m. to 6:00 p.m.; Sunday, 9:00 a.m. to 8:00 p.m. Admission is $4 for children ages 3 to 12. Adults and children age 13 and up are $8. Zoo hotline: (612) 432-9000.

Museum of American Art, in the Landmark Center, 75 West Fifth Street, Saint Paul, 55102. Open Tuesday to Saturday from 11:00 a.m. to 4:00 p.m.; Thursday, 11:00 a.m. to 7:30 p.m.; Sunday 1:00 to 5:00 p.m. Admission is free. (612) 292-4336

Museum of Questionable Medical Devices, 219 SE Main Street, St. Anthony Main, Minneapolis, 55414. Open daily except Monday. Admission is free. (612) 379-4046

Nicollet Island, located in the Mississippi River. Get there via the Hennepin Avenue Bridge.

Nicollet Mall, located between Washington Avenue N. and 12th Street S. in downtown Minneapolis.

Nokomis-Hiawatha Regional Park, located on Minnehaha Parkway. Lake Nokomis is on the south side and Lake Hiawatha is on the north. Open year round. Admission is free.

Northrop Auditorium, 109 Northrop Auditorium, 84 Church St., SE, Minneapolis, 55455. Open Wednesday to Saturday from 8:30 p.m.; Sunday 7:30 p.m.; Wednesday and Thursday matinees are 1:30 p.m. Admission varies. (612) 624-2345

The Ordway Music Theatre, 345 Washington St., St. Paul, MN 55102. Presents outstanding theater, ethnic dance and musical groups. Home of the internationally renowned, St. Paul Chamber Orchestra. Hours: Usually runs Tuesday to Sunday. Admission is $8 to $70. Tickets, (612) 224-4222

The Penumbra Theatre Company, Martin Luther King Center at the corner of Kent and Ingleheart; 270 N. Kent Street, St. Paul, 55102. Open from August to June with five main-stage shows. Admission is $14 to $17. (612) 224-3180

Phalen-Keller Regional Park, Highway 61, Maplewood, 55109. Phalen beach is open Memorial Day to Labor Day. Cross-country ski trails are open from December to mid-February. Recreation center is open during the summer from Monday to Friday 10:00 a.m. to 9:00 p.m. Admission is free. (612) 777-1707

P.J. Asch Outfitters, 413 Nelson Street, Stillwater, 55082. Open Monday to Friday. Admission is $5 to $7. Equipment Rental is $8. (612) 430-2286

Rain Forest Café, first floor, Mall of America. (612) 854-7500

Rice Park, between Fourth and Fifth Streets and Washington and Market Streets in downtown St. Paul. Open year round. Admission is free.

St. Anthony Falls, between Hennepin Island and the I-35 West bridge in the Mississippi River at Minneapolis.

Saint Paul Gangster Tours, 827 Portland Avenue, St. Paul, 55104. Tours depart from the St. Paul Hotel at 350 Market Street one Sunday a month at 12:00 p.m. Admission is $18 for adults, $15 for children ages 6 to 15. Kids age 5 and younger are free. (612) 292-1220

The Schubert Club Musical Instrument Museum, 75 W. Fifth Street, St. Paul, MN 55102; (612) 292-3267. Open Monday through Friday, 11 a.m.–3 p.m. Admission is free.

Science Museum of Minnesota, 30 East 10th Street, St. Paul, 55101. Open Tuesday to Saturday from 9:30 to 9:00; Sunday, 10:00 to 9:00. Omnitheater and Exhibit hall combination pass is $7 for adults, $6 for children ages 4 to 12. (612) 221-9444

Spoon Lake, between Keller Lake and Gervais Lake in St. Paul with entrances at Arcade Street and Keller Parkway.

Starbase Omega Laser Tag, 318 South Avenue, Mall of America, Bloomington, 55425. Admission is $8 to $22. Open Monday to Thursday from 10:00 a.m. to 10:00 p.m.; Friday to Saturday, 10:00 a.m. to 11:00 p.m.; Sunday, 11:00 a.m. to 8:00 p.m. Call for mission times. (612) 858-8015

State Theatre, 805 Hennepin Avenue, South, Minneapolis, MN 55402. Performance times vary. Admission ranges from $15 to $67. (612) 339-7007

Stone Arch Bridge, spans the Mississippi River between Lock and Dam #1 and the I-35 West bridge.

Target Center, 600 First Avenue North, Minneapolis, 55403. Hours and admission vary. Call (612) 673-1313 or TicketMaster 989-5151.

Taste of Minnesota, see Calendar, for July.

Teatro Latino de Minnesota, 3501 Chicago Avenue, S., Minneapolis, 55407. Hours vary. Admission is $8 to $12. (612) 432-2314

Theodore Wirth Regional Park, off Highway 55 on Theodore Wirth Parkway, Minneapolis, 55415. Open year round. Admission is free.

↑ Fishing at Theodore Wirth Regional Park

Thompson's Family Fun Center, 3013 27th Avenue S., Minneapolis, 55406. Open Tuesday to Saturday from noon to 11:00 p.m.; Sunday, 3:00 to 11:00 p.m. Admission is $1.75. All games operate on nickels. (612) 722-7474

3M, 3M Center, Maplewood, 55119. (612) 733-1110

TicketMaster, (612) 989-5151

Tourism Hotlines, Minneapolis, 370-9103; St. Paul, (612) 222-1000

Trains at Bandana Square, 1021 Bandana Boulevard, East St. Paul, 55108. Open Monday to Friday, 10:00 a.m. to 8:00 p.m.; Saturday, 10:00 a.m. to 6:00 p.m., Sunday, noon to 5:00 p.m. Admission is $2 per family. (612) 647-9628

Valleyfair Amusement Park, One Valleyfair Drive, Shakopee, 55379. Open daily from Memorial Day to Labor Day and most weekends in May and September. Admission is $20.95; $4.95 for children age 4 to 4 feet tall. (612) 445-7600

Walker Art Center and Minneapolis Sculpture Garden, on the corner of Lyndale and Vineland at 725 Vineland Place, Minneapolis, 55403. Open Tuesday to Saturday from 10:00 a.m. to 5:00 p.m.; Sunday, 11:00 a.m. to 5:00 p.m. Closed Mondays. Admission is $4 for adults and $3 for students; free for kids age 12 and younger. No admission charge every Thursday and the first Saturday of each month. (612) 375-7577

Willard Munger State Trail, connects Keller Regional Park in St. Paul with Pine Point Park near Stillwater.

World Trade Center and City Center, 33 S. 6th Street, Minneapolis, 55402. Open Monday to Friday from 9:30 a.m. to 8:00 p.m.; Saturday, 9:30 a.m. to 6:00 p.m.; Sunday, noon to 5:00 p.m. (612) 372-1200

ANSWERS TO PUZZLES

page 3

```
R O B U S K I D E Q L B A I G F X
K O A U Q K A E S O P C Y P V U K
D P H W R D I S Y M F L Y I N G D
R Y N L S G R I N N W M C Y L T Q
I T P O D Q P K A E I P A U S U I
V A T S G M L R E V C W M T U D E V
I M A P M E A R G N E N P T I E I V
N D S R T U N N H E I G I E T W V
G A X O P C E N R K C L N R C D G
A O H D U K R F W B A A G F A Q
U I S E I S U R N P Y D N V S U F
R T O U R I S T E T A X I Y E F
```

page 11

page 13

The word "Pioneers is missing from the sculpture's plaque.

page 21

page 23

page 25

```
K O N A T K M E S O P M (P A R K) H
(F) P H F R D Q S Y M (B) E B A O N H
(L) Y N (H) A G A I N (F I S H) B L T F
(O) T P O I S S K A T R N G E L T D
(W) A T J G K N R D V D E L T R D (G)
(E) E U E M A I N G N S C G E Y E (A)
(R) D S R G T N N H U Y U C E B W R
(S) A N S P I I N G C C N M R A D (D)
(P O N D) U N R O I B O N T F L Q E
 U I S E I G U B N C Y D N L L U (N)
 R O T B L K I T E U L I M Y N F E
(S A I L B O A T) F R A P B X E Q R
```

page 29

page 35

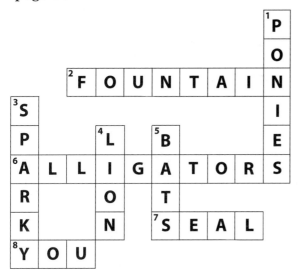

page 37

page 47

page 51

page 53

page 55

page 61

page 63

```
              1G
         2I N D O O R 3S
     4B      C          A
  5L A S E R          A  F
     L       S        D  F
     L       K        S  E
                      P
             6G O L F
                      R
     7B A T           R
           8E V E N T S
             S
```

page 65

page 73

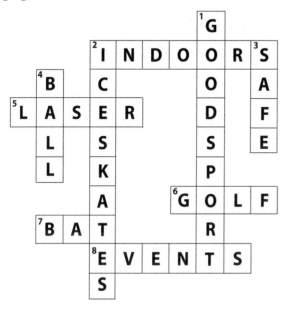

page 75

page 79

page 81

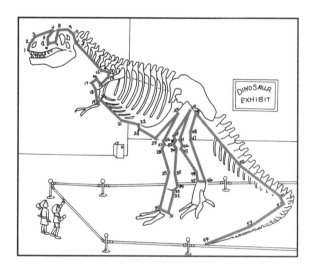

page 87

page 89

page 91

```
S O N A T K M E O S(S C E N E)V U H
S P H F R D Q(A U D I E N C E)N H
P O Y N L(A C T O R S)E T S B L T F
O T T A D O D R S K A U I N G U L U T
L I A A W G M N R G V S E N T E D I
I E N E M D F O G N T I G T Y E C
G D A C I R G U L N H U A U N E B W K E
H O N D N K R O W B E A T F I Q T
T U I G O I S U R N P Y D N L L N B
R O M B(C U R T A I N)I M Y N F G
D Y D N I O P Y F R I S(P L A Y)R
```

page 97

page 95

134

page 103

page 105

page 107

GEOGRAPHICAL INDEX: WHERE IS EVERYTHING?

Hudson Road, Sunray
Café Latte
The Carousel restaurant
Children's Theatre Company
Como Park Zoo and
  Conservatory
Gervais Lake
Harriet Island playground
Indian Mounds Park
Inside Sports
Keller Lake
Kohlman Lake
Lake Phalen
The Malt Shop
Minnesota State Fair Grounds
Phalen-Keller Regional Park
Round Lake
St. Thomas University
Spoon Lake
Trains at Bandana Square
Willard Munger State Trail

North Suburbs

Bridgeman's restaurants:
  Brooklyn Center
  Columbia Heights
Broadway Pizza:
  Coon Rapids
  Crystal
  St. Anthony
Circus Pizza:
  Blaine
  Brooklyn Park
Fuddruckers restaurant:
  Snelling Avenue

Gibbs Farm Museum
Kahn's Mongolian Barbeque
Lava Links

South Suburbs

Bloomington Ice Garden
Bridgeman's restaurants:
  Apple Valley
  Inver Grove Heights
  Richfield
Broadway Pizza restaurants:
  Apple Valley
  Richfield
Chutes and Ladders playground
Circus Pizza restaurants:
  Burnsville
  Edina
  South St. Paul
Fort Snelling Historic Site
Fort Snelling State Park
Fuddruckers restaurants:
  Bloomington
  Burnsville
Grand Slam Sports
Mall of America:
  Golf Mountain
  Knott's Camp Snoopy
  Rainforest Café
  Starbase Omega
Minnesota Air Guard Museum
Minnesota Valley National
  Wildlife Refuge
Minnesota Zoo
Valleyfair
West St. Paul

East Suburbs

All Seasons Golf Dome
Bridgeman's restaurant:
  North St. Paul
Broadway Pizza:
  Woodbury
Lake Elmo Park
P.J. Asch Outfitters
3M

West Suburbs

Bridgeman's restaurant:
Brooklyn Center
Broadway Pizza:
  Hopkins
  Plymouth
  Robbinsdale
Child's Play Theatre Company
Circus Pizza:
  New Hope
Edinborough Park
Eloise Butler Bird Sanctuary
Fuddruckers:
  St. Louis Park
Theodore Wirth Regional Park

INDEX

PHOTO CREDITS

from John Muir Publications

American Origins Series

Each is 48 pages and $12.95 hardcover.
Tracing Our English Roots
Tracing Our German Roots
Tracing Our Irish Roots
Tracing Our Italian Roots
Tracing Our Japanese Roots
Tracing Our Jewish Roots
Tracing Our Polish Roots

Bizarre & Beautiful Series

Each is 48 pages, $14.95 hardcover,
$9.95 paperback.
Bizarre & Beautiful Ears
Bizarre & Beautiful Eyes
Bizarre & Beautiful Feelers
Bizarre & Beautiful Noses
Bizarre & Beautiful Tongues

Extremely Weird Series

Each is 32 pages and $5.95 paperback.
Extremely Weird Bats
Extremely Weird Endangered Species
Extremely Weird Fishes
Extremely Weird Frogs
Extremely Weird Reptiles
Extremely Weird Spiders
Extremely Weird Birds
Extremely Weird Insects
Extremely Weird Mammals
Extremely Weird Micro Monsters
Extremely Weird Primates
Extremely Weird Sea Creatures
Extremely Weird Snakes

Kidding Around™ Travel Series

Each is 144 pages and $7.95 paperback.
Kidding Around Atlanta (avail. 1/97)
Kidding Around Cleveland (avail. 2/97)
Kids Go! Denver
Kidding Around Minneapolis/St. Paul
Kidding Around San Francisco
Kids Go! Seattle
Kidding Around Washington, D.C.
  (avail. 2/97)

Kids Explore Series

Written by kids for kids, each is $9.95
paperback.
**Kids Explore America's African
  American Heritage**, 160 pages
**Kids Explore America's Hispanic
  Heritage**, 160 pages
**Kids Explore America's Japanese
  American Heritage**, 160 pages
**Kids Explore America's Jewish
  Heritage**, 160 pages
**Kids Explore the Gifts of Children with
  Special Needs**, 128 pages
**Kids Explore the Heritage of Western
  Native Americans**,
  128 pages

Masters of Motion Series

Each is 48 pages and $6.95 paperback.
How to Drive an Indy Race Car
How to Fly a 747
How to Fly the Space Shuttle

Rainbow Warrior Artists Series

Each is 48 pages, $14.95 hardcover,
$9.95 paperback.
Native Artists of Africa
Native Artists of Europe
Native Artists of North America

Rough and Ready Series

Each is 48 pages and $4.95 paperback.
**Rough and Ready
  Homesteaders**
Rough and Ready Cowboys
Rough and Ready Loggers
**Rough and Ready Outlaws and
  Lawmen**
Rough and Ready Prospectors
Rough and Ready Railroaders

X-ray Vision Series

Each is 48 pages and $6.95 paperback.
Looking Inside the Brain
Looking Inside Cartoon Animation
Looking Inside Caves and Caverns
Looking Inside Sports Aerodynamics
Looking Inside Sunken Treasure
**Looking Inside Telescopes and the
  Night Sky**

Other Children's Titles

Habitats: Where the Wild Things Live,
  48 pages, $9.95

**The Indian Way: Learning to
  Communicate with Mother Earth**,
  112 pages, $9.95

Ordering Information

Please check your local bookstore for
our books, or call **1-800-888-7504** to
order direct and to receive a complete
catalog. A shipping charge will be
added to your order total.

Send all inquiries to:
**John Muir Publications
P.O. Box 613, Santa Fe, NM 87504**